FORTIFIED

FORTIFIED

The Affluent's Guide to Protecting Wealth,
Lifestyle, and Legacy

BENJAMIN WALKER

Contents

For my wife, Amanda. Thanks for loving me even when I spent more time talking your ear off about writing this book than I did actually writing it.

And for my children, Adam, Sam, Tristan, Ashton, Quinn, and Oliver. You are the wealth I treasure, the lifestyle I cherish, and the legacy I will leave.

Introduction

If you had asked me as a child what I wanted to be when I grew up, "Insurance Advisor" wouldn't have cracked my top 100. From a young age, I'd had dreams of making my way out to Hollywood to create movies. I love films and even then, longed to be a part of making them.

But life has had a funny way of steering me toward the work I was actually meant to do, which turned out to be very different. My path into insurance was complete happenstance — and funnily enough, had a lot to do with smells.

Let me explain. In early 1996, I took a job at Kentucky Fried Chicken. Though not my first job, it's where I consider that my working life began. "All the free chicken you can eat!" my friend Chris told me as we sat in our high school photography class. He wanted me to come work with him, and he knew he had me at free fried chicken. I started as a cook at $4.25 per hour, which was insanely low even then. But I quickly learned that the Colonel's Secret Recipe was less about the 11 herbs and spices and more about hard work and elbow grease. Within four years, I had climbed the ladder from chicken cook to Owner-Operator of my own KFC.

(The chicken was not all-you-can-eat, by the way.)

The KFC years changed my life in so many ways. During that time I got my first apartment, got married, and welcomed my first two kids into the world. But Hollywood is no place for a young family, so that dream was set aside. Life was moving fast, and my little family was just trying to hang on. But after a few years, the long hours, the missed holidays, and — worst of all — going home every night smelling like fried chicken and grease traps had burned me out. We decided it was time for a change. So with gratitude and a touch of fear, I sold my stake in the restaurant and at age 22, enrolled in college to pursue a law degree.

Going from young business owner to starving student wasn't easy. We had to cut our family budget to make it through school, and one of the first things to go was our movie money. As I said, I love movies, so naturally, my solution was to get a job as a manager at the local cinema while putting myself through school, where the movies were free, and the popcorn bucket was bottomless.

The next few years were a blur — college classes by day, movie theater by night, and somehow still managing to be present for my growing family as we welcomed kids numbers three and four. I earned my Associate's Degree from Utah Valley University and was accepted to Brigham Young University to finish my undergrad, still chasing that law school dream. But between 18-credit-hour semesters and full-time work, the strain on me, my marriage, and my kids was becoming impossible to ignore.

When the cinema chain asked me to manage theaters full-time and in another state, I faced a difficult decision. The combination of a less-packed schedule, less stress, and more money meant we might be able to repair some cracks that had started to appear in our marriage, so for the sake of the family, we agreed to set the law school dreams aside.

Managing theaters took us from Utah to New Mexico to Virginia. I loved the work, but the pattern was familiar — long hours, missed holidays, working weekends, and yes, coming home smelling like the job. This time, popcorn instead of fried chicken.

Then in 2007, my father suffered a mini-stroke. Being thousands of miles from family suddenly felt unbearable — not just for me, but for all of us. So when the opportunity to return to Utah came, we took it. My father recovered and lived another decade. My marriage, however, did not. It barely lasted another year.

For two years, I stepped into the life of a single father, raising four kids on my own. Those were the hardest years — but they also clarified what mattered. I realized that, unfortunately, the theater world amplified all the reasons I'd left KFC: the hours, the weekends, the holidays missed. I was back at another crossroads.

Somehow in that difficult stretch, I found time to start dating again — something I hadn't done since high school. Eventually, I met Amanda and convinced her to marry me. I don't know what she was thinking, saying yes to a divorced dad of four in the middle of yet another career crisis, but I'm grateful she did.

Around the same time, my sister Kathi, an insurance agent for a national insurance company, told me about an open position at one of their branches. My first question: "What do you smell like when you go home at night?"

Her response: "Money."

I was sold. Or at least sold enough to give it a shot — even though at the time, insurance seemed… well, dull. Numbers, forms, quotes, *premiums*. A necessary part of adult life, not exactly a calling. But as I settled into the work, something in me shifted.

I still remember the day Paul walked into the office. He was mid-40s, with weathered hands and work boots held together with duct tape. His visit wasn't to shop for a better rate as I'd assumed. Instead, he sat down across from me and said, "I need someone to look at my policy and help me understand the coverage I actually have."

Paul told me about his brother, Jason, and sister-in-law, Nicole, whose home had caught fire the year before due to an electrical issue in the garage. The family got out safely, but the house was a *total loss*. They had insurance, of course, and they had paid premiums for 15 years without filing a claim. It had seemed reasonable to assume they were covered. They weren't. Not really.

Their policy had been written as a *landlord policy* by their agent because, at the time the policy was written, Jason and Nicole were using the home as a rental property. They had temporarily moved from their home in Utah to San Antonio so Jason could attend dental school. On returning to Utah and moving back into their home, it didn't occur to them to contact their insurance agent to have the policy rewritten as a *homeowners policy*. Their agent could have spotted this had they held annual policy reviews, but sadly, the opportunity was missed.

After the fire, Jason and Nicole learned that their landlord policy lacked several essential coverages that a homeowners policy would have provided. For starters, they had no loss-of-use coverage to provide temporary housing while their home was being rebuilt. Landlord policies replace this coverage with loss-of-rental-income coverage, but because they were living there themselves, Jason and Nicole weren't collecting any rent. With only $3,000 in *personal property coverage*, there wasn't much to replace the belongings that had been destroyed. Landlord policies generally provide very little coverage for personal property because, typically, furnishings in a rental belong to the tenant. And lastly, they had no *extended replacement cost* coverage to help cover any shortfall in the home's rebuild cost.

"They're still recovering," Paul told me. "This set them back by several hundred thousand dollars, and Jason still works overtime every week trying to dig themselves out of the hole. Nicole had to go back to work to help with finances." He paused and shook his head. "They thought they had done everything right. But they missed one small detail, and they didn't have anyone looking out for them who could have caught it."

Looking up to catch my eye, he said, "My insurance isn't something I want to cheap out on. I just want to know my family's actually protected and that someone I can trust is watching out for me."

Paul wasn't looking for a salesman that day. He wasn't looking for the lowest premium or the fastest quote. He was looking for someone to sit with him, go through the fine print, and build solid protection with and for him. That's when it hit me that he needed me to be that someone.

I spent over two hours with him. We went through everything. I showed him where his coverage was solid and where it had gaps. We made changes, some of which cost him more, and some that just required better documentation of what he owned. By the end, he knew exactly what he had and exactly what to expect if the worst happened. When he stood up to leave, he shook my hand and said, "I wish my brother had talked to someone like you."

Click!

Insurance isn't about paperwork. It's about people and their sense of security. About protecting the homes, livelihoods, and lifestyles that families like yours work so hard to build.

Insurance may not be as sexy as Hollywood — but protecting people is. That realization changed everything.

My job at the insurance company, however, was to sell insurance, which I performed very successfully. Period. Pam, another agent in my office, and I were reminded of that by management one day as we had spent a bit too long consulting with existing clients rather than selling to prospects. "The 800-number is for service guys! Let the service center answer their questions, and you guys get back to your sales calls!"

Within six weeks of that chat, Pam and I had quit and co-founded our own agency, Custom Insurance Solutions, where we could offer clients access to many insurance carriers and be the advisors they deserved. Pam and I built the agency together on the principles of honesty, stewardship, exceptional service, and genuine expertise. We ran it together for nine years, until Pam retired happily in 2020. Looking back now, what strikes me most isn't the growth of the business in that time — it's the change I've watched happen in the people we've served.

Over the years, I've observed many clients move from ambivalence or ill regard toward insurance to genuine engagement and relief, simply because someone finally explained it in a way that made sense. I've seen anxiety turn into confidence as we built plans together that truly matched their exposure. I've watched people sleep better because someone had their back. (Okay — I didn't really watch them sleep. That would be disturbing and wildly inappropriate for a Risk Advisor.)

As I developed expertise and built relationships in the industry, I was recruited to work with families whose complexity matched my curiosity. These families had significant wealth, multiple properties, collections, businesses, and exposures that standard insurance couldn't begin to address. Now the stakes were higher. The risks more intricate. But the core mission remained the same: helping people protect what they'd built.

In working with high-net-worth clients, that spark became a full-blown sense of purpose. I've seen firsthand how success multiplies risk. How wealth brings freedom — but also exposure. And how even the most successful families can feel vulnerable because no one's ever shown them the full picture.

The more estates I've walked through, the more stories I've heard, the more passionate I've become about helping people protect what matters most. Instead of being about just policies sold, it became about stewardship. About creating clarity and calming the chaos that success can often create.

Some people are born into their calling. Others, like me, trip face-first into it and discover it fits better than anything they'd imagined. So, no, insurance wasn't the childhood dream. But helping people? Building trust? Keeping families protected from the unexpected? That was always the dream. I just didn't know where it would lead.

And now, years later, I'm exactly where I'm supposed to be — advising families, creating clarity, and turning complexity into confidence. Even writing this book. Not because the world needed another generic book about insurance, but because this book didn't exist.

There are plenty of technical manuals written for insurance professionals. Stacks of basic guides for first-time homebuyers. But there's almost nothing for families like yours — people who have built something significant and who need to understand how to protect it.

This book exists to reframe how you think about insurance — not as a transaction or a box to check and forget about, but as a critical tool in a broader risk management strategy. To give you the clarity to ask the right questions, spot the gaps, and make informed decisions about protecting everything you've worked for.

You don't need to become an insurance expert. But you do deserve to understand your own risk — and to have someone in your corner who's shown you the full picture.

Welcome to Fortified.

Let's protect what you've built.

Getting the Most
Out of This Book

Now that you know why I wrote this book, let me tell you how
to use it.

What This Book Will – and Won't – Do

This book provides a framework for thinking about risk that I
call the Four Pillars of Risk Management, and it can be
applied to every area of your life. It will walk you through the
specific exposures that matter most to affluent families: your
homes, vehicles, collections, household employees, liability,
legacy, and more. For each area, it will explain the questions to
ask and the typical gaps.

By the time you finish this book, you'll have a much clearer
understanding of your risk profile than you have now. You'll
know what to look for, and you'll be able to have more
informed conversations with advisors and evaluate whether
they're truly serving you.

What this book won't do is turn you into an insurance expert.
You'll still need qualified *risk advisors*. In fact, in reading this,
you may realize the advisors you have aren't cutting it. Nor

will this book give you specific policy recommendations. What works for one family might be completely wrong for another. The principles here are universal; the applications are personal. That's why no book — including this one — can replace a good advisor who actually knows your situation.

What I'm offering is informed confidence. Not the false confidence that comes from assuming everything's fine because you're paying premiums. Real confidence — the kind that comes from genuinely understanding your situation and making intentional decisions about how you go about protecting the people and things in your life that mean the world to you.

Reading This Book

Chapter 1 explores what changes when your wealth crosses into territory that requires you to think differently. Chapter 2 introduces a practical framework that you'll apply throughout the rest of the book. Read these two chapters first, regardless of which specific topics concern you most.

From there, the book moves through specific risk areas.

- The homes you love
- The vehicles that move you
- The finer things you collect
- The increased exposure at your level
- The household staff
- Cybercrime and other emerging digital threats
- Family and legacy
- International considerations

Each chapter ends with the Fortified Framework — a practical summary of how to apply the Four Pillars to that topic. Use these as checklists when reviewing your own coverage.

You'll also find a helpful Glossary in the Appendices at the back of the book. Wherever you find italicized terms in the chapters, it means that you'll find the explanations in the Glossary.

You can read straight through or jump to chapters relevant to your immediate situation. Both approaches work.

One important suggestion before we get going: wherever you start, bring your advisors into the conversation. Share what you're learning. Use the frameworks to guide discussions. A good advisor will welcome an informed client. One who feels threatened by your knowledge may not be the right partner for the fortified life you're building.

The Invisible Line

The Paradox of Success

Blindsided

I'll never forget the day Mark and Angie walked into my office. They were in their early 50s, well-dressed, and arrived in a car that cost more than their first home. They'd built a thriving software company from nothing — late nights, big risks, and a lot of grit. They'd sold it a few years earlier for eight figures, paid off the mortgage on their dream home in the mountains, bought a second place on the coast, and finally felt like they could breathe.

Then came the demand letter.

Their longtime housekeeper claimed wrongful termination after they let her go due to ongoing performance issues. She alleged age discrimination, emotional distress, and unpaid overtime. In the demand letter, her attorney requested $150,000 in damages. Mark made two initial calls: first to his attorney, and then, on their recommendation, to his homeowners' insurance company. After talking with a claims adjuster and reviewing the policy terms, he discovered it didn't cover domestic employment-related liability at all. Neither did their *umbrella policy*, leaving them exposed to potentially hundreds of thousands in defense costs and settlements.

Mark and Angie weren't reckless; it simply hadn't occurred to them that this type of exposure existed, and they surely hadn't known that this was something they could have insured against. Yet there they were, facing the reality that their success had changed their exposure and could be a costly lesson.

Stories like Mark and Angie's are more common than you think. There's a moment many successful families experience when wealth stops being only a reward and instead creates new vulnerabilities. It's known as the *Threshold Effect* — that invisible line where your net worth, lifestyle, or visibility changes the rules of risk. Cross that line, and the strategies that protected you on the way up will no longer be much help.

Understanding the Threshold

When your net worth is modest, risk management is relatively straightforward. A standard homeowners policy, an auto policy, maybe a small umbrella — done. You're insured. You could practically handle it during a lunch break. (I miss those days.)

But as wealth grows, so does complexity. You acquire more homes, more vehicles. Maybe some art, jewelry, and a wine collection. Then you need household staff. You're offered board seats, perhaps even start to take an interest in philanthropy. Or build a public profile that makes you recognizable. Of course, you'll travel to remote corners of the world. Suddenly, the exposures multiply, and the stakes rise dramatically.

Here are just a few ways the risk landscape shifts:

Asset volume and diversity: You might think that a $5 million home would be twice as risky as a $2.5 million home. It's not. It's exponentially more complex. Rebuilding costs, unique architectural features, high-value contents, and location-specific *perils* (wildfire, earthquake, flood) can all come into play.

Liability attractiveness: Success makes you a target. Plaintiffs' attorneys know that a judgment against someone with visible wealth is more collectible. Frivolous claims become more likely — and more expensive to defend.

Lifestyle exposures: Private aircraft, yachts, exotic travel, or even hosting large events at home introduce risks that standard policies never have to contemplate.

Family and legacy complexity: Trusts, blended families, children with their own assets, or philanthropic commitments create interlocking exposures that a single overlooked detail can unravel.

Visibility and reputation: In today's world, wealth often comes with a digital footprint. A single negative story, true or not, can damage reputations built over decades.

The threshold isn't a fixed dollar amount. For some families, it hits at around $5 million in investable assets. For others, it might be closer to $10 million or $25 million. It's more about the nature of your life than the number on a statement. But once you're there, pretending the old rules still apply is one of the biggest risks of all. Mark and Angie learned this the hard way.

Risks in Plain Sight

Most of the families I work with aren't careless. They're diligent, responsible, and proactive in most areas of their lives. Yet the same blind spots consistently emerge when it comes to protecting themselves.

Assuming "more coverage" equals "better protection," Many people address the question of adapting to their growing wealth by simply increasing the limits on their existing policies. But standard policies have structural limitations, such as *exclusions*, *sub-limits*, and definitions, that don't scale with affluence.

Receiving fragmented advice: You likely have a team that includes a wealth manager, a CPA, an estate attorney, and an insurance broker. No doubt each is excellent. But risk doesn't respect silos. In the spaces between advisors, vulnerabilities can develop.

Mistaking activity for coverage: Paying large premiums may feel like protection. It's easy to assume that because the bills are high and the policies are thick, that everything is handled. But paying more doesn't guarantee you're covered correctly.

Ignoring emerging risks: Cyber extortion, climate-driven catastrophes, social media defamation, *employment practices* claims by household staff — these weren't significant concerns 20 years ago. They are now.

These blind spots aren't character flaws among those experiencing the threshold effect. They're the natural consequences of success outpacing the systems designed to protect it.

Mark and Angie's experience with the housekeeper lawsuit is a perfect illustration. Like so many of my clients, they discovered too late that employing domestic staff introduced liabilities that their standard policies simply didn't address. Yet this felt like a natural part of an affluent lifestyle. They were smart, careful people who worked with an established advisor to arrange coverage they believed was right for them. Their problem was failing to recognize that their success had moved them into a different risk category.

The Emotional Toll

You've worked hard to provide security for your family, so naturally want to enjoy the fruits of that labor without constant worry. Yet many of my clients confess they lie awake wondering, "Am I really protected? Or is there something big I'm missing?" That unease isn't paranoia. It's intuition telling you that your world has changed, and you probably need to do something about it.

That initial shock hit Mark and Angie hard. It wasn't just financially; it was emotionally. Mark told me later that it felt like the ground had shifted under his feet. But that anxiety doesn't have to be a permanent feature of your life. It can be contained and greatly reduced by understanding the full extent of your exposure.

Crossing the Threshold with Eyes Open

Rather than fearing the threshold effect, treat it like any other practical challenge. To deal with it, you need to understand it. Once you do, you stop reacting and start intentionally designing protection. That's where the real freedom lies, not just in having wealth, but in knowing it's truly safeguarded.

We'll return to Mark and Angie in Chapter 7, "The Household Enterprise," where we'll look at how families can properly structure and insure the people who help run their homes. For now, their story serves as a clear example of how quickly a blind spot can turn into a serious exposure.

Take the Personal Risk Audit

Before reading further, consider completing the Personal Risk Audit in the Appendix. It will help you identify which chapters are most urgent for your situation — and which gaps need immediate attention. A fillable PDF version is available at www.fortifiedbook.com/resources.

In Chapter 2, we introduce the framework that guides every discussion in this book: the Four Pillars of Risk Management. Risk Reduction, Risk Transfer, Risk Avoidance, and Risk Retention — these four principles apply to every exposure we'll cover, from your homes and collections to your liability and legacy. Master them, and you'll move from vague unease to genuine confidence.

2

The Fortified Framework

You know that moment in *Rocky* when Bill Conti's song "Gonna Fly Now" kicks in? Seen running through the streets of Philadelphia, Rocky's training for his title shot against Apollo Creed, and by the time he hits those museum steps, it already feels like a victory — even though the fight hasn't happened yet. That feeling isn't accidental. In the score, the horns build, the percussion pushes forward, the tempo climbs right alongside Rocky — every element of the music is working together toward that triumphant peak. Everything has been constructed with intention.

That score was written specifically for Rocky, for that moment, for that story. It wouldn't work the same way in a different film. The music lands because it was composed to fit Rocky's journey — mirroring the early morning runs, the doubt, the long climb, and the eventual breakthrough. The structure serves the story it was written for. I must have watched that scene 100 times before I stopped just feeling it and started hearing what was happening beneath the surface. The structure makes the emotion possible because of the intentionality that underlies it.

After helping thousands of families navigate their insurance and risk exposures, I have come to realize that a truly well-designed risk management plan is built the same way — not off the shelf, but composed specifically for you, for your life, for this stage of your journey.

A Soundtrack to Accompany Your Life

Think of your risk management plan as a musical composition designed with the life you're living right now in mind. Like any great piece of music, it needs both structure and freedom: a framework that holds everything together and room for the melody to become yours uniquely.

This structure comes from what I call the Fortified Framework — and its four pillars: *Risk Reduction. Risk Transfer. Risk Avoidance. Risk Retention.*

These pillars are like the key and time signatures of your composition — they're the underlying architecture that keeps everything coherent. They hold the music together, measure after measure, year after year. But within that structure, the notes on the page are yours — shaped by every home you acquire, every vehicle you love, every passion you pursue, every responsibility you shoulder. And they should change as your life changes.

There is no such thing as a typical structure. A young executive building wealth requires a different mix than someone who is preparing to pass a legacy to the next generation. A homeowner in wildfire country needs fire-resistant landscaping written in from the start, whereas the recurring themes for a collector of rare art will include tailored provisions for storage and security. And the requirements of someone with teenage drivers inevitably differ from those of the empty-nesters next door, enjoying their retirement years.

The notes that belong in your composition depend entirely on the life you're living right now — not the life you lived five years ago, and not some generic template that worked for someone else. As with musical notes, essential features must be combined in bespoke, innovative ways. For example, a renovation changes your property's exposure, so it also requires a policy redesign. Equally, increasing your international travel frequency will intersect with liability concerns. I'm certain you currently hold multiple policies to cover these things. Those policies will either harmonize or create dissonance. When these elements are composed thoughtfully, they strengthen the entire piece. When they're thrown together without intention, the music suffers.

A fortified life isn't about playing it safe or keeping the music small. It's about composing something that lets your life resonate fully — without the fear that one unexpected note will bring the whole piece crashing down. When the structure is sound, and the composition fits *your* life, your wealth doesn't just survive the unexpected. It flourishes.

The Four Pillars: A Closer Look

Behind every resilient family and high-performing household lies a common framework built on four timeless principles that guide every decision. They're not complicated, but they are powerful. Let's examine them one by one:

Risk Reduction: Mitigate What You Can

Risk reduction is about minimizing the likelihood or impact of *loss* through preparation, maintenance, and awareness. For a homeowner, it might mean upgrading to a fire-resistant roof or installing an automatic water shutoff system to avoid catastrophic damage later. Similarly, a collector might choose to add climate control to a wine cellar or secure their valuables in a proper safe. Or, where household staff is involved, the family would want to conduct background checks, maintain their alarm systems, and establish clear communication protocols.

This pillar removes luck from the equation and replaces it with readiness. You can't prevent every loss, but you can make them less likely and less severe when they occur. Every dollar spent on thoughtful prevention can save thousands — sometimes hundreds of thousands — when things go wrong.

The Stray Ember

The Martins learned this lesson through a $50,000 claim — and the months of frustration that followed. They'd built a beautiful outdoor fire pit, positioned about 20 feet from their pool house. What they hadn't considered was prevailing wind patterns or the value of a simple spark screen. One windy April evening, an ember from the fire pit traveled those 20 feet and ignited the roof of the pool house, which was a total loss. Their insurance covered the rebuilding costs, but coverage doesn't erase consequences. The Martins were out of pocket their $25,000 *deductible*. Reconstruction took nearly five months, leaving them without the pool house they'd designed for entertaining for an entire summer. Yet a $200 spark screen could have prevented the entire loss. They would have discovered this in a conversation with their insurer's risk management team, which would have been available to them at no additional cost.

Risk Transfer: Share the Burden Wisely

Risk transfer is the process of shifting financial responsibility to someone else — usually an insurance carrier, though it can also be achieved through contractual agreements. When you buy insurance, you're not just purchasing peace of mind. You're purchasing potential liquidity — the ability to recover without disrupting your wealth, your plans, or your family's future. You pay a known, manageable amount of money in advance (the premium) to avoid an unknown, potentially catastrophic amount in the future (the loss).

But insurance isn't the only transfer mechanism. Contracts with vendors and service providers can include indemnity clauses that hold them responsible for their own mistakes — and, in turn, their insurers. For example, if a plumber is servicing your in-sink garbage disposal and forgets to tighten the fitting back on, and as a result, the next time you run your dishwasher, the hose pops off, flooding your kitchen and ruining your hardwood floors, an indemnity clause in your service agreement would ensure that they are liable to make you whole and repair the damage. Requiring certificates of insurance from anyone who works on your property isn't paranoia; it's risk transfer hygiene.

Remember, though, that the goal isn't to transfer every risk, but to transfer the risks that would be catastrophic if they materialized.

Trust But Verify

The Nolans learned a hard lesson on what happens when risk transfer fails. They had several mature oaks along their property line, two of which caused concern. They were leaning noticeably toward their neighbor's home and were within range of hitting it if they were to fall in a windstorm. The family's landscaper suggested it was time to bring in a professional to remove them, since they were far too large for him to handle. The tree removal company they hired came highly recommended by a friend, offered a reasonable quote, and could start the following week. The Nolans knew enough to ask the tree company whether it was licensed and insured, and were assured it was.

Midway through the job, one of the large oaks fell the wrong direction. It crashed through the roof of the neighboring home, destroying a section of the second floor and seriously injuring the neighbor, who was home at the time. Emergency crews and insurance adjusters descended on the quiet cul-de-sac within hours. The neighbor sued both the tree removal company and the Nolans. When the Nolans' attorney contacted the contractor's insurer, they discovered the business owner's policy had lapsed four months earlier due to non-payment. The contractor had no assets to speak of. Suddenly, the Nolans were the only defendant with resources — and they became the sole target of the litigation.

What should have been the contractor's problem became a six-figure nightmare for the Nolans, dragging on for nearly two years before a settlement was reached. The financial damage was significant. The relationship with their neighbor was destroyed. And all of it could have been avoided if they had required the contractor to provide a *certificate of insurance* before work began. Contractors routinely provide these for commercial clients, but individuals rarely think to ask. Hiring a professional tree-removal service was the Nolans' attempt to shift the risk from them and their landscaper, but risk transfer only works if the other party can bear it.

Require certificates of insurance dated within the last 30 days. Ask to be named as an *additional insured* on the contractor's policy — this ensures you'll be notified if coverage lapses. Just 10 minutes of due diligence can save you years of litigation and hundreds of thousands of dollars.

Risk Avoidance: The Art of Choosing Not To

Avoidance is the silent pillar — and it's often the hardest for high achievers to accept.

It means recognizing when the risk isn't worth taking. There are times when choosing not to serve on a nonprofit board with vague bylaws and inadequate *directors and officers coverage* is by far the best option, even if it seems tempting. Perhaps you should say no to the exotic pet that would create insurance nightmares. Sometimes the sophisticated choice is simply to say no.

But avoidance requires discernment, not fear. Some risks are worth taking because the activities bring joy, meaning, or fulfillment. The goal isn't to avoid everything that carries exposure because that would make for a small, constrained life, and that's not what wealth is for. The goal is to avoid risks with unfavorable ratios: high potential downside, limited upside, and exposures that can't adequately be reduced or transferred.

Consider whether to buy a trampoline or not. They're among the highest-liability items a homeowner can have (other than that time you tried deep-frying that Thanksgiving turkey), and most insurers won't cover homes that have them if the yard isn't fully fenced, and/or lacks a safety net enclosure. If your children desperately want a trampoline, the question to ask isn't whether it's risky — it is. So, is the joy worth the residual risk after you've reduced what danger you can (enclosure nets, supervision rules, proper installation) and confirmed you can transfer what remains (your insurer will still cover you)? Sometimes the answer is yes. Sometimes the answer is visiting a trampoline park instead, where someone else bears the liability.

Avoidance isn't about fear. It's about making intentional choices.

Risk Retention: Own What Makes Sense

Some risks are worth accepting. Some exposures are too small, too predictable, or too manageable to outsource. Risk retention in these cases means choosing what you will effectively self-insure — and preparing to do so. It might mean carrying a higher *deductible* on your policy, covering minor losses out of pocket, or maintaining liquidity specifically for predictable expenses. The key is deciding what your approach will be in each case. This is intentional ownership, not passive acceptance.

The wealthy have an advantage here. You have the capacity to absorb losses that would devastate others, which means you might choose to retain more risk and pay less in premiums. A $10,000 deductible might be catastrophic for a young family, whereas for you, it may be a mere annoyance. The premium savings over time often exceed the occasional out-of-pocket expense.

Risk Calculus

The Parkers had always carried low deductibles —
$1,000 on their home, $500 on their vehicles. It felt like
the safe choice. But during an annual review, I asked
them a different kind of question: "How much risk are
you willing to self-insure?" They had ample resources.
What they didn't fully appreciate was that making low-
dollar claims can hurt you more than the payout benefits. Every claim goes on your record.

Too many claims — even small ones — can lead to
non-renewal, higher premiums, or difficulty finding
coverage elsewhere. That $1,500 kitchen leak you filed a
claim for might cost you far more in long-term insurability than if you'd simply handled it out of pocket. I
suggested they restructure their coverage with this in
mind. We raised their home deductible to $25,000 and
their auto deductibles to $2,500. Yes, their annual
premiums dropped by $7,000 — but that wasn't the
primary goal. The higher deductibles served as a
natural deterrent to making small claims, a way to
balance risk and reward, and a recognition that insurance should be reserved for what it's designed for:
significant, unexpected losses.

Over the next five years, they had two incidents that
would have been claims under their old structure: a
minor fender bender and a roof leak over a guest bath-
room. Total out-of-pocket cost: $11,500. Total premium
savings: $35,000. But more importantly, their claims
history remained clean, their insurability intact, and
their relationship with their carrier strong. The net
benefit was more than $23,000 — plus the knowledge

that their retention was intentional and strategically sound.

But retention has limits. Some risks should never be retained regardless of wealth: catastrophic liability exposure, risks with unlimited downside, and anything that could threaten your family's financial foundation. Retain what would be inconvenient. Transfer what would be devastating.

"Retain what would be inconvenient. Transfer what would be devastating."

How the Four Pillars Work Together

These principles don't compete; they complement one another. The strongest risk strategies use all four in balance.

- Reduce what risks you can.
- Transfer risks that would be catastrophic.
- Avoid what risks you can live without.
- Retain what risks you can comfortably absorb.

RISK MANAGEMENT STRATEGY SCALE

CONSEQUENCE

LIKELIHOOD		INSIGNIFICANT	MINOR	MODERATE	MAJOR	CATASTROPHIC
	ALMOST CERTAIN	Low/Medium	Medium	Medium/High	High	High
	LIKELY	Low	Low/Medium	Medium	Medium/High	High
	POSSIBLE	Low	Low/Medium	Medium	Medium/High	Medium/High
	UNLIKELY	Low	Low/Medium	Low/Medium	Medium	Medium/High
	RARE	Low	Low	Low/Medium	Medium	Medium

RETAIN	TRANSFER	REDUCE	AVOID

Fig. 1: Where do the risks in your life fit in the matrix? Consider how likely they are and what the outcome would be if they occurred.

Reading the Scale

The ratings suggest which pillar should guide your approach:

Low — Retain. These risks are unlikely to occur and would cause minimal damage if they did. Self-insure them. Accept that small losses happen, and don't waste premium dollars or mental energy on exposures that won't meaningfully affect your life. A scratched bumper, a broken window, a minor appliance failure — handle these out of pocket and move on.

Low/Medium — Transfer or Retain. These risks warrant a decision. They're either somewhat likely with minor consequences or unlikely with moderate consequences. Consider whether the cost of transferring them (through insurance or contract) is worth the peace of mind — or whether you're comfortable absorbing the loss if it happens. Your liquidity and risk tolerance should guide the choice.

Medium — Transfer. These risks sit in the middle of the matrix — likely enough and consequential enough that you shouldn't carry them alone. This is the core territory for insurance: events that probably won't happen, but would hurt if they did. Transfer the financial exposure to a carrier and remove the uncertainty from your life.

Medium/High — Reduce and Transfer. These risks are serious. They're either highly likely or highly consequential — sometimes both. Transferring them isn't enough; you should also take active steps to reduce the likelihood or severity. Install protective systems. Implement safety protocols. Maintain your property. Then transfer whatever residual risk remains.

High — Avoid or Reduce Aggressively. These are the risks that keep advisors up at night. The consequences would be severe, and the likelihood is uncomfortable. If possible, avoid the exposure entirely — don't buy the asset, don't engage in the activity, don't take the position. If avoidance isn't realistic, reduce the risk as aggressively as you can and ensure you've transferred what remains with appropriate limits. Never leave high risks unaddressed.

When you face any risk, run through these questions:

1. Can this risk be reduced? What preparation, design, or prevention would make it less likely or less severe?
2. Can this risk be transferred? Is there insurance available? Can contracts shift responsibility appropriately?
3. Should this risk be avoided? Is the exposure worth the benefit? Are there alternatives with better risk-reward ratios?
4. Should this risk be retained? Is it small enough to

absorb? Would transferring it be prohibitively expensive?

As you move through the chapters ahead, you'll see these Four Pillars everywhere. They govern how you protect your properties, select your vehicles, manage your collections, structure your household, and prepare your family for the unexpected. From now on, every chapter will conclude with a Fortified Framework section that applies these four principles to that chapter's specific risks.

Once you've internalized this framework, every decision becomes clearer. Risk management shifts from reactive — scrambling to respond after something goes wrong — to a more strategic approach. You'll even find this empowering. No longer hoping you're protected, you'll know precisely how each risk is being addressed, which pillar is doing the work, and where the boundaries of your protection lie.

Your life is the melody. It's complex, evolving, and uniquely yours. To keep it the way you planned it, let the Four Pillars be the rhythm. And when rhythm and melody align, when every element knows its role and plays its part, your wealth doesn't just survive the unexpected. It flourishes.

In Chapter 3, we turn to the most valuable asset most families own: their home. When starter homes become dream estates, everything about protecting that asset changes. Let's explore how to fortify the place where your life really happens.

3

There's No Place
Like Home(s)

"Be it ever so humble…" isn't that what they say? Well, maybe that could have been said about your first home, but your home now — or homes — is a far cry from that. Whether you bought it or built it, your home is of your making and has become your Fortress of Solitude. It is also likely one of your largest personal assets. Properly protecting it needs to be a vital part of your overall risk management plan.

But your homeowners insurance is more than just property protection. It's the linchpin in your entire insurance program — covering not just the structure itself, but your personal liability, personal property (at home and around the world), legal defense, guest medical, employment practices liability, cyber exposure, and much more. The coverage that flows from your primary residence policy reaches far beyond the walls of your home.

Many of these areas are important enough to have earned their own chapters ahead. For now, let's focus on protecting your home's physical structure and ensuring that, if the worst happens, it can be restored with the craftsmanship it deserves.

The Problem with Standard Coverage

Standard homeowners policies were designed for standard homes. Cross into high-value territory, and they start breaking down in ways that aren't obvious until you need to file a claim.

More than half of the policies I review for new clients are underinsured, often by millions. The causes vary from policies that haven't been updated after renovations, cost-per-square-foot formulas that simply don't work for custom builds, or agents who don't understand high-value homes and try to shoehorn them into policies that don't fit. Often, it's a combination of all of the above.

The result is families who think they're protected — they're paying premiums, they have a policy — but who would face a six- or seven-figure gap if they ever needed to rebuild. One such case is Tom's. Let me tell you about him.

The Whale

Tom was referred to me by his business partner, Bryant, in early 2022. He complained that he was paying a fortune for his homeowners insurance and wanted to explore his options. Tom and his wife had built a 21,000-square-foot home in 2019, featuring high ceilings, custom finishes throughout, a home theater, a gym, two pools, and an elevator. His policy provided just over $4 million in *dwelling coverage* — that's $190 per square foot — for a luxury custom-build.

When Tom asked his agent whether this was sufficient, the agent replied, "Most losses aren't a total loss anyway," and that the policy included extended replacement cost coverage. I found that clause in his policy; it was only an additional 25 percent. Four million plus 25 percent is five million. That's still only $238 per square foot. A luxury custom build is easily double that and can be many multiples higher without breaking a sweat. "Could you rebuild it for that?" I asked. Tom went pale. "It cost me $9 million to build in 2019 — not counting the land. And that was pre-pandemic."

Our conversation shifted entirely. This wasn't about paying too much anymore. It was about being dangerously underinsured. His loss-of-use coverage was capped at 24 months — not nearly long enough to rebuild a home like his. Personal property coverage was limited to $2 million, which didn't account for his art and wine collections. *Other structures coverage* was capped at $400,000, nowhere near enough to cover his pool house, guest house, or two pools.

We wrote a new policy with a *private client carrier*. Tom's home was now insured for just over $9 million under a *guaranteed replacement cost* policy with no cap. *Loss of use* became actual loss sustained. The outbuildings and pools were appropriately covered. And the new package — with more than double the coverage — cost less than he'd been paying before. I don't know whether Tom's agent was earnest but negligent or whether Tom's account had grown to be the whale of the agency and the agent simply didn't want to let it go. Either way, the result was the same. A family exposed to millions in potential loss, paying premium prices for inadequate protection.

Why Private Client Carriers Are Different

Private client coverage isn't just standard coverage with higher limits. It's built differently from the ground up — designed for homes that can't be rebuilt from a catalog.

Standard carriers know how to replace *a* house. *Private client carriers* know how to restore *your* house.

The difference matters when it's time to rebuild. The imported tile in your kitchen may come from a single artisan in Portugal. The millwork throughout may require craftsmen whose skills are increasingly rare. The architect who designed your home may need to be involved in reconstruction. A standard carrier's claims process isn't built for this. They're thinking about comparable materials and efficient contractors. A private client carrier understands that "comparable" isn't the same as "what you had."

Extended Replacement Cost

Most standard policies offer "extended replacement cost," which typically pays 25-50 percent above your stated coverage limit, though some leave it off entirely. That 25-50 percent above what's calculated sounds generous until you need it. As Tom discovered, his 25 percent extension still left him $4 million short.

Guaranteed Replacement Cost

Guaranteed replacement cost works differently. It's typically based on a professional appraisal done at your property, not in a piece of estimation software that can't capture the custom nature of your home. If you experience a loss, the carrier pays the actual *reconstruction cost*, regardless of limits. No running out of funds and no disputes during a crisis.

If guaranteed replacement cost is available to you, take it. This single feature can be the difference between full restoration and painful compromise. On occasion — especially for homes in challenging locations such as unprotected mountain areas or regions prone to wind or named-storm damage — even private client insurers may not offer it. But even then, they start with a replacement-cost figure based on their appraisal and years of experience restoring luxury homes after a loss.

Other Key Differences

Beyond guaranteed replacement cost, private client policies typically include:

- **Loss of use coverage that's unlimited** for as long as necessary. A property loss becomes an inconvenience, not a lifestyle catastrophe. This alone can be worth the entire premium difference.
- **Dedicated claims professionals** who specialize in high-value properties have the authority to make decisions and return calls the same day. They work with your preferred contractors rather than forcing you into impersonal carrier networks.
- **Broader coverage forms** are built on inclusion rather than exclusion, meaning fewer gaps and coverage for situations the policy drafters didn't anticipate.

Property Protection

Coverage	Private Client	Standard Market
Guaranteed Replacement Cost	Full rebuild Cost, No Cap	125-150% of Dwelling Coverage
Cash-Out Option	Included	Not Available
Guaranteed Contents Replacement Cost	Included	Not Available
Identity Fraud/Financial Fraud	Available	Not Available
Large Loss Deductible Waiver	Waived over $50,000	Not Available
Sewer/Drain Backup	Up to Dwelling Value	Available but Limited
Equipment Breakdown	Full Coverage	Limited
Primary Flood Coverage	Available	Not Available
Food Spoilage	Included	Not Available
Wildfire Defense	Active Protection Services	Not Available
Home Valuation Consultation	Included	Not Available
Loss Prevention Guidance	Included	Not Available

Other common coverage differences between private client carriers
and the standard market. Note: Coverage features, limits, and
availability vary by carrier and state.

Carrier Investment in Prevention

Private client carriers have always offered risk management
services — complimentary home appraisals, security assessments, and wildfire consultations, to name a few. But in recent
years, they've moved beyond advice into active prevention.
The best claim is one that never happens, and carriers are
increasingly willing to invest to make that true.

"The best claim is the one that never happens."

Increasing Requirements

Many private client carriers now require protective systems as
a condition of coverage. Central station fire and burglar
alarms. Automatic water shut-off devices that detect leaks and
stop them before a drip becomes a flood. Electrical system
monitors that identify *hazards* before they cause fires. Temperature sensors that alert you when heating fails, and pipes are at
risk of freezing.

These requirements aren't arbitrary. Water damage is the most common cause of homeowners claims, and a single undetected leak can cause hundreds of thousands of dollars in damage. Electrical fires destroy homes that could have been saved with early warnings of bad wiring. Carriers have learned that homes with these systems file fewer claims — and when they do, the losses are smaller.

Expanding Incentives

It's not all stick, though. Carriers are also introducing plenty of carrots to help improve your home fortification in several ways:

- Premium discounts for homes with qualifying protective systems. The savings can be substantial enough to offset installation costs over time.
- Post-loss installation programs that pay for protective systems after a related claim. If you experience water damage and an automatic water shut-off device could have prevented or reduced it, or if you experience a break-in and an alarm system could have prevented it, some private client carriers will pay to install the device or system to prevent a recurrence.
- Proactive installation programs can provide warning systems before any loss occurs. Some carriers now offer complementary loss-mitigation devices to their policyholders, such as Ting, which plugs into a standard electrical outlet and monitors your home's electrical system for hazards that can lead to home fires—often detecting problems weeks before they would otherwise be discovered. By providing loss-prevention devices at no cost, carriers know that preventing one fire saves far more money than the cost of thousands of devices.

For more on Ting, water shut-off devices, and other loss prevention systems, visit www.fortifiedbook.com/resources

Your carrier is heavily invested in ensuring you do not experience a loss. But you should be even more invested. These systems protect your home, your belongings, and your family — not just the carrier's loss ratio.

I occasionally see clients push back on these requirements. They don't want the cost or inconvenience of installing an alarm or water shut-off device, yet they still expect the carrier to offer a policy and pay out a claim when something goes wrong. Some carriers will decline coverage entirely if you refuse to meet their requirements. Don't let resistance to these requirements cost you access to the best carriers. Also, don't wait until it's a requirement. If your carrier recommends protective systems, embrace them. You're not doing the carrier a favor. You're protecting what matters most to you.

Beyond Your Primary Residence

If you own additional properties, including vacation homes, rental properties, or investment real estate, each requires consideration. The same principles we discussed for your primary home apply, but with a few nuances. Here are some things to know about your other properties:

Secondary Homes

Vacation properties carry different risks than your primary residence. Key considerations:

- **Rental use.** Do you rent the home out when you aren't there? If you rent your property — whether occasionally through Airbnb (Short-term) or on a long-term basis — your carrier needs to know.

Different rental arrangements require different coverage. A policy written for owner-occupied use may not respond to a claim that occurs while renters are in the home, unless the carrier is aware of the renters and a "Rented to Others" *endorsement* is added. That's why you should verify what coverage you have before listing the property for rent.

- **Monitoring and caretakers.** The monitoring systems we discussed earlier become even more critical — and more likely to be required — for secondary homes. Distance compounds problems. A small leak goes undetected for weeks when you're not there. Remote monitoring systems — water sensors, security cameras, temperature alerts — can notify you before small problems escalate into catastrophic ones. Local caretakers who regularly check on the property can catch what sensors miss. Many carriers require these arrangements for secondary homes as a condition of coverage, not just an incentive.
- **Seasonal perils.** Your mountain cabin faces different risks than your beach house. Winterization matters in cold climates. Hurricane season matters on the coast. Wildfire season matters in dry regions. Make sure your coverage addresses the specific perils each property faces.

Investment Properties

When you own property as an investment rather than a residence, the policy type changes entirely. Investment properties need landlord policies, not homeowners policies.

The differences are significant. *Loss of rental income* replaces loss of use — this reimburses you for rent you can't collect while the property is uninhabitable, not paying to house you elsewhere yourself. Personal property coverage is minimal because landlord policies assume the tenant is responsible for their belongings. Liability exposure differs because tenants and their guests create different risks than owner-occupied situations.

Remember Jason and Nicole from the Introduction? Their home caught fire, and they discovered their landlord policy didn't provide the coverage they needed, because they were living in a property insured as a rental. The reverse is equally problematic: insuring a rental property with a homeowners policy. Match the policy to the property's use.

Holding investment properties in LLCs can create separation between property liability and personal assets — worth discussing with your attorney if you own multiple properties.

Additional Considerations and Coverages

No matter how you own or how you use a properties, there are some common considerations to keep in mind:

Contractor Due-Diligence

Across all properties, verify that contractors carry valid insurance. Remember the Nolans from Chapter 2? They hired a tree removal company that claimed to have insurance but didn't. When a neighbor was seriously injured, the Nolans became the sole target of litigation. Require certificates of insurance. Verify they're current, and ask to be named as an additional insured.

Coordination

Families often end up with a patchwork of policies from different carriers, each with its own terms. And usually through different agents. The better approach is to have all properties insured through the same carrier or private client program whenever possible. What they need are consistent forms, coordinated limits, gaps not missed, and simpler administration.

Additional Coverage: What Your Policy Doesn't Include

Even a well-structured homeowners policy inevitably contains gaps. Certain perils are excluded by default and require separate coverage. These apply to your primary residence — but don't forget to consider them for secondary and investment properties as well.

Flood Insurance

Standard homeowners policies don't cover flood damage. If you want flood protection, you need a separate policy.

The National Flood Insurance Program (NFIP) provides federally backed coverage, but it has significant limitations for high-value homes. Dwelling coverage caps at $250,000. Contents coverage caps at $100,000. Basement contents are largely excluded. And claims processing can be slow.

For homes that exceed these limits, there are two options. *Private flood insurance* offers higher limits, broader coverage, and often faster claims handling. Excess flood insurance sits above an NFIP policy and provides additional limits once the federal coverage is exhausted.

Don't assume you're safe just because you're not in a high-risk zone. A significant percentage of flood claims come from properties outside designated flood areas.

Earthquake Coverage

Earthquake damage is excluded from standard homeowners policies. If you're in a seismically active region, such as California, the Pacific Northwest, or parts of the Midwest, earthquake coverage is essential. Policies are available as standalone coverage or endorsements, typically with higher deductibles (often 10–20 percent of the dwelling limit). Even outside obvious earthquake zones, the cost of coverage is often reasonable and worth considering.

Equipment Breakdown

Modern homes rely on complex systems: HVAC, elevators, generators, smart home technology, wine cellars with climate control, and pool equipment. When these systems fail due to mechanical or electrical breakdown, not from an external cause such as fire or lightning, standard policies typically don't respond. That's when equipment breakdown coverage fills this gap. Some private client carriers include it automatically; others offer it as an endorsement.

To close out this chapter, let me tell you about the Williamses.

The Claim That Went Right

The Williamses show what happens when coverage and prevention work together. Blake and Amy owned a 7,500-square-foot custom home featuring imported stone, smart home systems throughout, and a 2,500-square-foot detached guest house.

When they came to me, we discovered together that their current plan was severely exposing them, so we restructured their entire approach.

Risk Reduction: They invested in a whole-home water leak detection system with automatic shut-off. They also upgraded their electrical panel after an inspection revealed aging components. Importantly, they documented everything — photos, videos, receipts for every improvement, and appraisals for valuables.

They used their carrier's complimentary risk management services, including a wildfire assessment that led to better vegetation management around the property.

Risk Transfer: Blake and Amy moved to a private client carrier with a replacement cost of $4.2 million, a guaranteed-replacement-cost loss settlement, and unlimited loss-of-use coverage. To be on the safe side, they added separate flood coverage even though they weren't in a high-risk zone.

Risk Avoidance: When the Williamses considered adding high-liability features to their property, such as a rock-climbing wall and a shooting range, we walked through the coverage implications, and they made informed decisions about which exposures to accept and which to avoid.

Risk Retention: By raising their deductible to $25,000, Blake and Amy saved $4,500 annually in premiums. They maintained liquidity specifically earmarked for property-related deductibles and minor uninsured expenses. But then a kitchen fire filled their primary home with smoke, rendering it uninhabitable — mid-school year, with three kids at home.

Here's what happened next: Within hours, a claims specialist was assigned — someone with authority to make decisions on the spot. Within three days, the family was in comparable rental housing, covered entirely by their policy. When reconstruction bids exceeded the $4.2 million in coverage by $600,000, because construction costs had risen since the policy was written, their guaranteed replacement cost provision covered the difference. The 18-month rebuild restored their home to exactly what it had been — the imported stone, the custom millwork, the smart systems throughout, all down to the last detail.

The carrier's craftsman network connected them with contractors who understood the quality required. The rebuild wasn't a compromise. It was a restoration. Blake and Amy emerged without sustaining financial harm, without lifestyle degradation, and without an adversarial claims process. Yes, the fire was devastating. But because the right coverage and prevention measures were in place, they recovered completely. That's what fortification looks like.

The Four Pillars Applied to Homes

Risk Reduction

- Install protective systems: water shut-off, fire/burglar alarms, electrical monitoring
- Maintain proactive maintenance schedules
- Document everything: photos, videos, receipts, appraisals
- Use your carrier's complimentary risk management services

Risk Transfer

- Secure guaranteed replacement cost coverage

- Establish a correct replacement cost calculation based on a professional appraisal
- Confirm unlimited (actual loss sustained) loss of use coverage
- Add flood, earthquake, and equipment breakdown coverage where appropriate
- Coordinate coverage across all properties through one carrier when possible

Risk Avoidance

- Don't make unreported renovations or property changes
- Don't enter into unverified rental arrangements without proper coverage in place
- Don't resist carrier-required protective systems
- Don't let policies auto-renew without review

Risk Retention

- Choose deductibles intentionally based on your liquidity
- Maintain funded reserves for deductibles and minor uninsured losses
- Accept that it's often not worth filing claims for small losses

Your home is where your life happens. It deserves coverage that understands what makes it yours — and a carrier that knows how to put it back together.

In Chapter 4, we move from where you live to what you drive, sail, or fly. When the family sedan becomes a collection of vehicles consisting of luxury cars, classics, recreational equipment, and more — protecting them requires an entirely different approach.

————————————————

4

The Things That Blow
Your Hair Back (And
How To Protect Them)

————————————————

Whether your garage resembles Bruce Wayne's or you've just got a couple of SUVs and your teenager's first car in there, chances are it's a far cry from your early motoring days. Remember the car you drove when you were just getting started? The one you wouldn't be caught dead in now. You've clearly done something right because somewhere along the way, things changed. The garage filled up. The dock appeared. Maybe even a hangar. These assets represent freedom, passion, and real investment. Most importantly, they should bring you joy.

But they also bring a heightened level of risk. Without wanting to put a damper on things, the flashier vehicles can unfortunately signal a potential payday for an injured party or nefarious actor. And even the more modest ones pose a higher risk, simply because you have more to lose than you did back then. Let's look at a couple of instances that illustrate the difference some pre-emptive thinking can have.

Alone in D.C.

Megan was three months into her junior year at Georgetown University when she learned how quickly a nice car can make you a target. She was driving her Audi A7 — a graduation gift from her parents — through an unfamiliar part of DC when she felt the jolt of an impact from behind. On pulling over, she stepped out to find a large man in his mid-20s emerging from the other vehicle, followed by an equally intimidating passenger. Both men towered over her 5'4" frame.

Before she could speak, the man went on the offensive. He claimed *she* had stopped suddenly in front of *him* — essentially asserting that she had caused the accident. He demanded cash to settle it on the spot. She knew this wasn't the right way to handle the situation, but standing alone on that street, two strangers backing her against her own car, she didn't feel safe arguing the point. Nor did she feel safe calling the police in their presence. All she had on her was $350 in cash, so she handed it over. The men pocketed the money and drove off. No insurance exchange took place, and no contact information was provided. She'd been shaken down, and there was nothing she could have done about it.

Megan filed a police report later that day, but they never found him. The damage to the bumper wasn't awful, but it still cost just over $5,000 to fix. The real sting was that the body shop found her seat belt needed to be replaced due to the strain from the impact. After two weeks, the body shop called to let her know the bumper was fixed, but they couldn't legally release her car until the seat belt was replaced — and the part was on backorder from Germany.

Nine months. That's how long Megan waited to get her car back. Most auto insurance policies cap rental coverage at somewhere around $30–50 per day, for up to 30 days. Fortunately, we had placed Megan's family in a policy with $15,000 in *rental reimbursement* and no time limit. She ended up having to keep that rental car longer than some people keep their own cars. Without that coverage, her family would have paid nearly $12,000 out of pocket just for her rental. Over a seat belt.

Shawn's case wasn't as scary as Megan's, but we still found gaps that could have cost him tens of thousands of dollars.

He's Got a Fast Car

Shawn found me after seeing some of my marketing. Although he was not unhappy with his old insurance carrier, he thought a conversation would be worthwhile. Once we started talking, it soon became clear what he really wanted to discuss: his garage. He was a car enthusiast in the truest sense with three daily drivers, plus a Rolls-Royce Ghost and his pride and joy — a Ferrari 488 Spider. I asked to see his auto insurance policy. I found everything was covered at *Actual Cash Value* (ACV). Every vehicle. Including the Ferrari. Here's what that would have meant if Shawn had totaled the Ferrari under his old policy: an adjuster would have searched for "comparable sales" — except there's no such thing as a comparable 488 Spider. They're rare. They're hand-built. Those that do sell vary wildly based on options, year, mileage, condition, and timing.

The adjuster might have found one that sold for $220,000. Maybe $195,000. Shawn would have been handed a check for whatever number the carrier decided was fair — and invited to sue if he disagreed. That's not a hypothetical. That's how ACV works. You don't find out what your car is "worth" until after you've lost it. By then, of course, you have no leverage. We moved Shawn to *agreed-value coverage*, which meant he and the insurer agreed on the replacement value upfront. The Ferrari was insured for $280,000 — period. Not "up to" $280,000. Not "approximately" $280,000. Exactly $280,000. The Rolls-Royce and his daily drivers got the same treatment. The new policy also included original manufacturer parts, worldwide liability, and physical damage coverage on rental vehicles abroad.

A few months later, Shawn and a friend were heading to their country club for lunch in the Ferrari when he mistimed a yellow light and hit a car in the intersection . Thankfully, the impact wasn't catastrophic, and no one was hurt, but the Ferrari was a write-off. Under his old policy, Shawn would have faced a five-figure gap between what he'd lost and what he might recover. On top of that, there would be months of negotiation. Maybe litigation. He would have been entirely exposed — after the fact — to a definition of "value" he never agreed to. Instead, the adjuster just asked one question: "Where would you like your $280,000 sent Shawn?"

These stories reveal a lot about the unpredictable nature of vehicle ownership. What follows is a breakdown of where exposure lives — in your garage, at your marina, and in your hangar.

Part One: Road Vehicles

Daily Drivers and Luxury Vehicles

Your daily drivers may not be the most exciting vehicles in your garage, but they're where you have the most exposure. Every mile driven is an opportunity for an accident.

At $100,000 per person and $300,000 per accident, many affluent drivers are still carrying policy limits that were inadequate even 20 years ago. A catastrophic accident can generate claims in the millions. If your limits are $300,000 and you cause an accident with $800,000 in damages, the other $500,000 comes from your assets.

Uninsured/Underinsured Motorist coverage (UM/UIM) is no less critical. If someone with minimum insurance limits injures you, your own UM/UIM coverage pays what they can't. Match UM/UIM to your *liability limits* — always. It's one of the most cost-effective types of coverage available, and why would you insure others better than you insure yourself and your family?

Megan's story raises another question about rental car coverage after a crash. When your Ferrari is in an accident like Shawn's, what rental vehicle do you want while yours is being repaired? Would you settle for driving a Ford Escape to the country club? Or even a Mustang? Make sure that your auto policy has like-kind rental coverage.

Collector, Classic, and Exotic Vehicles

Shawn's story illustrates the problem: standard policies use ACV, which means there is inevitable post-loss negotiation between owner and insurer over what a "comparable" vehicle would cost. For rare and exotic vehicles, however, there may not be a comparable. You need agreed value coverage, which is established upfront and paid in full upon a total loss.

This is a dynamic market, so you'll need to review agreed values annually. The collector market can move dramatically. A car valued at $150,000 five years ago might be worth $300,000 today — or $100,000. Your coverage should reflect the current reality.

Track days create a specific gap because standard auto policies — even collector policies — typically exclude racing or timed events. If you plan on participating in high-performance driving events, you'll need coverage that addresses this activity. If you show up at the track and assume your regular coverage applies, it could cost you hundreds of thousands of dollars in the event of a crash.

Recreational Vehicles

Golf carts, ATVs, dirt bikes, and snowmobiles can be enjoyable for sure, but they can also present exposure that's often left uninsured. Standard auto insurance doesn't cover most recreational vehicles, and homeowners might provide limited liability coverage, although usually only when used on your property.

Start by making an inventory of each recreational vehicle you own at every property. Determine explicitly what coverage is available for each, because off-road vehicles require their own policies that provide liability, physical damage, and *medical payments coverage*.

Vehicles

Coverage	Private Client	Standard Market
Coverage Territory	Worldwide	U.S. and Canada only
Valuation Method	Agreed Value	Actual Cash Value
Lease/Loan Gap	Included	Typically Not Available
Collector Vehicles	Available	Typically Not Available
Parts Used in Repairs	OEM When Available	Aftermarket Permitted
Rental Car Coverage	Up to $15,000, No Daily Cap	Up to $1,500 with Daily Limit
Personal Property in Vehicle	Up to $2,500	Not Available

Note: Coverage features, limits, and availability vary by carrier and state.

Part Two: Watercraft

From jet skis to yachts, watercraft create exposures that differ fundamentally from land vehicles. This is why marine insurance can be its own specialized world.

Hull Coverage and P&I

Hull coverage is what protects a vessel against physical damage. For larger or high-value watercraft, agreed value coverage is essential — watercraft don't depreciate like cars, and in some markets they even appreciate.

Navigation limits define where you can operate. Operating outside your limits can void coverage entirely. If your cruising plans include waters not covered by your policy, adjust coverage before you go. I've seen clients plan a trip to the Bahamas only to discover, fortunately before departure, that their policy stopped at territorial waters.

Then there is Protection and Indemnity (P&I), which is marine liability coverage. It covers *bodily injury* to passengers and third parties, property damage to other vessels and docks, wreck removal costs, and pollution liability. For a day boat, $500,000 might be adequate. For a larger yacht, $1-5 million is more appropriate, depending on size and use.

Charter and Crew

Chartering is considered a commercial activity, and personal yacht policies usually exclude commercial use specifically. This means that if you charter your watercraft and have a claim during that charter, your personal policy may deny coverage entirely. If chartering your watercraft is in the cards, consider obtaining a commercial watercraft policy before proceeding.

When your vessel has paid crew — even just a captain — you've entered maritime employment law. The *Jones Act* and maintenance-and-cure obligations for maritime workers create exposures that many yacht owners don't understand until a claim arises. This is worth exploring, as you may need separate crew liability coverage.

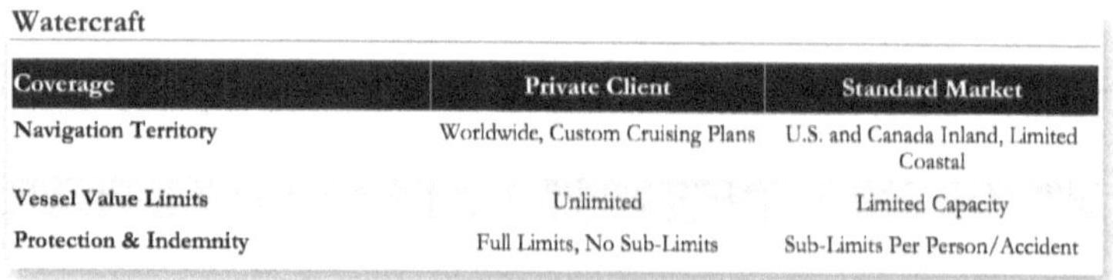

Watercraft

Coverage	Private Client	Standard Market
Navigation Territory	Worldwide, Custom Cruising Plans	U.S. and Canada Inland, Limited Coastal
Vessel Value Limits	Unlimited	Limited Capacity
Protection & Indemnity	Full Limits, No Sub-Limits	Sub-Limits Per Person/Accident

Note: Coverage features, limits, and availability vary by carrier and state.

Part Three: Aircraft

Who doesn't want to fly private? We'd all like to skip crowded airport security lines, avoid flight delays, and avoid being forced to sit in the middle seats. How about taking a spur-of-the-moment trip to Chicago for your favorite deep-dish pizza, or to New York to catch that Broadway show you just heard about? This freedom, though, comes with its fair share of unique exposures that require special care and planning.

Since you're reading a book by a specialized risk advisor for private clients, you may be surprised to learn that I am no expert in aviation insurance. I know just enough to be danger-ous, but I also know when even I need to call in a specialist. Aviation is one of those areas. When it comes to aircraft, I enlist pros who eat, sleep, and breathe aviation insurance — and you should too. If your insurance advisor isn't an aviation expert themselves, make sure they're collaborating with someone who is.

What I do know is that the Four Pillars still apply, so we'll soon break them down as they relate to your cars, watercraft, and aircraft.

But first, a quick primer on how aviation insurance is built. Unlike auto or homeowners coverage, aviation insurance pricing hinges on three key factors: *hull value*, time, and type. First, hull value is straightforward — it means what the aircraft is worth. Secondly, time refers to the pilot's experi-ence: total hours in the cockpit and hours they've spent in that specific aircraft type. Thirdly, "type" refers to the aircraft itself. A single-engine Cessna presents a very different risk profile than a twin-engine turboprop or a jet.

These three factors drive both your coverage options and your premiums. The good news is that aviation insurance usually becomes less expensive over time. As the hull's value decreases and the pilot spends more time in the cockpit, insurers typi-cally view it as a better risk. Just be sure to keep up on your annual insurance reviews to keep your policy updated.

Coordination and Specialists

When you have coverage for vehicles, watercraft, and aircraft, as well as an umbrella policy, their coverage can intersect in complex ways. Imagine a guest is injured on your yacht while docked at your waterfront home — would your yacht policy respond? Or would it fall under your homeowners policy?

Under what circumstances would your umbrella get involved? Proper coordination of policies ensures there are no gaps, and without it, you might find yourself in lengthy battles with multiple carriers while the claim goes unpaid. Crucially, luxury recreational assets require specialist brokers. A generalist may not have access to the right markets or know-how to navigate the nuances.

The Four Pillars Applied to Vehicles, Watercraft, and Aircraft

Risk Reduction

- Maintain everything to manufacturer standards — deferred maintenance can void claims.
- Invest in training: driver safety courses for young family members, high-performance instruction for exotic car owners, boating certifications, and recurrent flight training.
- Store high-value assets properly.
- Establish clear policies for who operates what, and stick to them.

Risk Transfer

- Carry liability limits appropriate to your net worth — at least $500,000/$1 million for most affluent families, and significantly higher for aircraft.
- Match UM/UIM to your liability limits.
- Use agreed value for any vehicle, vessel, or aircraft where ACV would leave you short.
- Ensure your umbrella policy coordinates with your auto, marine P&I, and aviation liability policies — not all umbrellas cover all three.

- For watercraft with paid crew, you may need separate crew liability coverage to address Jones Act and maintenance-and-cure obligations.
- For aircraft, verify pilot warranties are met, because operating with an unapproved pilot can void coverage entirely.

Risk Avoidance

- Be honest about usage when obtaining coverage and never operate outside policy limits or navigation boundaries. *Misrepresentation* can void policies.
- If you want to charter your watercraft, either get commercial coverage or don't charter.
- Obtain proper coverage beforehand if you do track days, or don't participate.

Risk Retention

- Choose deductibles commensurate with your ability to absorb losses. Higher deductibles will also reduce premiums, sometimes significantly.
- Evaluate whether physical damage coverage makes economic sense for lower-value assets. Retaining that risk might be rational.
- Never compromise on liability coverage. Physical damage to others' property is limited by the value of the damaged asset. Liability is not.

Your garage, your marina, your hangar — these achievements should represent the freedom that wealth provides. It's the Ferrari that makes you smile. The boat that holds your best family memories. And the freedom to fly according to your schedule.

These assets aren't just property. They're expressions of what you've worked for. With the right structure beneath them, they'll stay exactly that — sources of joy, not anxiety.

Protect them the way you built them — deliberately.

In Chapter 5, we examine another form of passionate ownership: collections. Whether it's fine art, wine, jewelry, or other valuables, protecting what you've curated requires its own expertise.

5

Collections, Curiosities, and Champagne Problems

Walk through any affluent home, and you'll see more than just furniture. You'll see the owner's passions. The art collected over decades, jewelry that marks milestones in their life — the engagements, anniversaries, and inheritances. Wine aging nicely in a cellar someone spent way too much time designing. Watches that cost more than some cars.

These things make a house yours. They mean something beyond the price they'd fetch at auction. Though let's be honest — that number matters too.

Despite this, standard homeowners insurance can treat all of it as an afterthought.

The Sub-Limit Problem

Your homeowners policy includes personal property coverage, usually calculated as a percentage of your dwelling coverage. For example, if your home is insured for $4 million, you might have $2 million in contents coverage. Sounds like plenty, right?

Look closer.

Buried in the fine print are sub-limits that cap pay-outs on specific categories and apply no matter how much total contents coverage you carry. Jewelry and watches? $5,000, maybe $10,000 if you're lucky. Fine art, same. Wine caps out around $2,500. Cash — and this one's almost funny — $200 to $500.

So, if you have $200,000 worth of jewelry, $300,000 of art, and $100,000 of wine, your sub-limits might cover... $20,000. The other $580,000? You're on your own.

The Quarter-Million-Dollar Burglary

Britta and Craig came to me after finding themselves sorely exposed.

They had been vacationing in Europe when professionals invaded their home. The thieves knew what they were doing when they took the jewelry and watches ($185,000), designer handbags ($75,000), and cash ($20,000) from the safe. Total loss: roughly $280,000.

Britta and Craig had done everything right. Or at least they thought they had. Appraisals, photographs, and receipts —all were organized and ready. They filed their claim and waited to be made whole. The insurance company paid them $12,500.

In other words, they received the combined sub-limit for jewelry, watches, handbags, and cash in their policy. Sadly, the remaining $267,500 was uninsured. All because they'd never scheduled their valuables and didn't even know their policy had sub-limits. Britta and Craig assumed "personal property coverage" meant their personal property was covered. It wasn't.

Thieves will know exactly the value of your possessions, even if your insurance policy doesn't.

Scheduling Items

Scheduling means listing specific items and their values in your policy. It pulls those items out of sub-limits entirely and covers them individually.

When you schedule a possession like your $100,000 necklace, it's covered for $100,000 — not $2,000. Itemizing your property assigns it agreed value coverage, which means no *depreciation* and no arguing about what it's worth if and when you file a claim. Most scheduled items carry no deductible, so you receive the whole amount back.

You'll pay for this service, of course. But the cost is reasonable at around $1–$2 annually per $100 of value annually. Your $100,000 jewelry collection might run to $1,000–$2,000 a year to schedule. Compare that outlay to having $100,000 in exposure protected by a mere $10,000 sub-limit.

For more modest valuables — say, under $100,000 in total — scheduling them under your homeowners policy is usually the simplest option. But once we're talking about significant collections, a standalone *collections policy* makes more sense. Also known as a *personal articles floater*, this policy provides better coverage, better claims handling, and terms designed for people who collect things.

Blanket Coverage

Some collections are simply too big to schedule piece by piece. If you owned 800 bottles of wine or a library full of rare books, you're not going to list every single item.

Blanket coverage handles this. To do this, you must schedule the collection as a whole: "wine collection, $200,000."

However, the trade-off is reduced precision, as blanket policies usually cap individual items. If you have a $200,000 wine blanket built into your policy, it might limit coverage for any single bottle to $5,000. Got a bottle worth more than that? Well, fine, but it needs its own line on the schedule.

For most serious collectors, a combination of blanket coverage and scheduling works best. Use blanket coverage for the bulk of the collection, then schedule the particularly valuable pieces individually.

Appraisals

Scheduling usually requires appraisals — although some private client carriers will take your word on items under $100,000. When appraisals are required, it's essential to use qualified, independent appraisers. That means GIA-certified appraisers for jewelry and specialists for art, wine, antiques, or collectibles. The jeweler who sold you the piece isn't necessarily the right person to appraise it for insurance purposes.

Update appraisals every two to three years, and more often if the market's volatile. That appraisal you had done five years ago probably understates what your piece is worth today.

Whatever you do, avoid skipping appraisals to save a few hundred dollars. A $300 appraisal that establishes your piece is worth $75,000 instead of the $50,000 you had guessed it would be worth equates to $25,000 extra in your pocket if you ever have to make a claim.

Category by Category

Fine Art

Art is complicated. Values swing based on auction results, critical opinion, changing tastes, and — let's be honest — whether the artist is still alive. Not only this, but coverage needs to include agreed value, restoration and conservation costs (which can run as high as the piece itself), coverage while in transit and on loan, *mysterious disappearance*, and accidental breakage.

The key is to document everything. Take photographs of the piece from multiple angles, including close-ups of signatures and condition issues, and of provenance records, certificates of authenticity, and condition reports from conservators. When a claim happens, you'll be glad you did.

Jewelry and Watches

This is the most stolen category because these items are small, valuable, and easy to fence. Descriptions matter here, so note down metal type and weight, stone specifications (cut, color, clarity, carat), and setting style for each piece. Again, take photographs from multiple angles.

Some carriers require that pieces with values above certain thresholds be stored in safes, so be sure to know your policy. Violating those requirements could affect your coverage when you need it.

Wine and Spirits

Wine needs specific conditions. Stable temperature and proper humidity, for starters, which is why coverage should explicitly include *spoilage* from climate control failure. That's a real risk, and it's not always covered automatically.

For large, active collections, documentation is ongoing and must be maintained. Cellar management software helps you track inventory as you buy, drink, and occasionally weep over bottles you should have opened five years ago.

The Wine Cellar

Several years ago, the Montoyas, my clients in Phoenix, approached me about their impressive wine collection. Containing roughly 3,500 bottles, it was valued at around $1,250,000 and housed in a climate-controlled cellar within their 9,500-square-foot home, which included a battery backup system.

When designing their insurance program, we discussed insuring the wine collection on a collections policy along with their jewelry and art. Most types of loss of a wine collection are already covered under a home-owners policy's personal property limit, but for wine, spoilage is typically limited.

I recommended the coverage. They told me that they understood the risk and chose to retain it. With such a great wine cellar, Phoenix's incredibly reliable power grid, and a battery backup system in place, the decision seemed reasonable at the time.

During a three-week trip away from home, a rare-for-Phoenix power outage on their block lasted four days. The backup battery was not designed for extended outages and failed after one day. Tragically, temperature swings destroyed most of the collection.

Because the wine had not been scheduled, the insurance recovery payment was limited to $2,500, a common sub-limit for wine spoilage.

Two things compounded the loss. First, the decision to retain that exposure; second, the system built to reduce the risk of a power-outage-related loss didn't account for such a prolonged service disruption. In other words, it was a risk reduction failure. Adding the wine to their collections policy would have cost a few thousand dollars a year and would have covered the entire loss.

It's a decision I think about every time I have the same conversation with a new client.

The Montoyas' story reminds us that risk retention is fine in some cases, but perhaps not for your most prized possessions.

Other Collectibles

Each type of collection follows specific conventions around how best to preserve and insure it. In a world of fakes and copies, sports memorabilia and collectibles need authentication from recognized services. More delicate items, such as rare books, require climate-controlled storage and specialized appraisers. Antique furniture can get tricky when people use it. Musical instruments, firearms, designer handbags — each has its own considerations.

If something has significant value and losing it would hurt, it needs specific coverage. Don't assume your homeowners policy handles it the way you would want it to.

Documentation

When you file a claim, you'll need to prove you owned the thing and can prove what it was worth. Photographs from multiple angles, video walkthroughs, receipts, current appraisals, certificates of authenticity, and condition reports all count. The more documentation, the better.

For safekeeping, store records somewhere other than your house. This might be a combination of cloud back-up, a safe deposit box, or copies with your advisor. Remember that the fire that destroys your art collection can also destroy the documentation proving you owned it.

Make this an annual ritual. Walk through with a camera, taking photographs as you go. Review your inventory and update appraisals for any values that have changed. Then, adjust your schedule. The whole process takes a few hours each year — hours that are worth every minute if you ever need to use the schedule.

Coverage Details That Matter

Mysterious Disappearance vs. Theft

Calling something a theft in the eyes of insurers requires evidence that a crime has occurred. That's why there's a category called mysterious disappearance that covers things that simply vanish — no forced entry, no witnesses, just gone.

This matters because professional thieves don't leave evidence. If your policy requires proof of theft and you can't provide it, you might have no coverage at all without scheduling.

The Disappearing Ring

Jill called me one day to say she hadn't seen her wedding ring in about five months.

She wasn't panicked. Because she split her time between three properties: her primary home in St. George, a beach house on Oahu, and a ski property in Aspen, Jill figured the ring would turn up eventually at one of them. It didn't.

We'd scheduled that ring for $85,000 on a collections policy along with her other jewelry. My team helped her file the claim, and because everything was properly scheduled, the carrier cut her a check for the full value of the ring. No hassle, no haggle, and no depreciation.

Life can be busy, and small items can be hard to keep track of. If it's of value to you, list it on your policy.

Breakage and Damage

There are times when things get damaged without being stolen. Make sure your coverage includes accidental breakage for these times, and understand how partial damage works— who decides whether to repair or replace? You or the insurance carrier?

Pairs and Sets

One of the most frustrating losses is to lose one of a pair. Lose one earring from a pair worth $60,000, and you'll find that some policies will only pay $30,000, half. Better policies cover the pair, recognizing that one earring alone is essentially useless. The same principle applies to china, silverware, and matched furniture, so choose your coverage wisely.

Newly Acquired Property

Most collections policies give you automatic coverage on new acquisitions for 30–90 days, up to a limited value. Don't let things sit unscheduled past that window. If you buy something significant, try to call your advisor that week to add it.

Working with Specialists

Many firms and private client insurance carriers also offer risk management services for collections. These include security assessments, storage recommendations, or guidance on transit and shipping. All these services help reduce the likelihood of claims. Use them.

Finally, make sure your collections coverage coordinates with everything else. Your personal articles floater should complement your homeowners policy. Liability exposure from collections is possible, especially when exhibiting it. Say someone trips over your sculpture that's on display at a gallery, or a guest is injured handling a piece you're displaying in your home. All these risks should be contemplated by your umbrella.

Collections & Valuables

Coverage	Private Client	Standard Market
Coverage Territory	Worldwide	Typically Not Available
Market Appreciation	Up to 150% of Scheduled Value	Repair/Replace Cost Only
Newly Acquired Items	90 days, 25% Per Class	35% or $10,000 Max
Transit & Exhibition	Available	Not Available
Diminution in Value	Covered	Not Available
Pairs & Sets	Full Value	Proportional Only
Mysterious Disappearance	Covered	Often Excluded
Borrowed Items	Up to $1 Million	Not Available
Collections Management	Included	Not Available

If you have spent so much money, time, and energy building your collection, why would you not protect it? Note: Coverage features, limits, and availability vary by carrier and state.

The Four Pillars Applied to Collections

Risk Reduction

- Employ safes, display cases, and alarms.
- Install climate control with back-up power for anything sensitive to temperature and humidity.
- Hire professionals to transport valuable collections. Don't move valuable art yourself.
- Install water leak detection near anything that mustn't get wet.

Risk Transfer

- Schedule everything significant and select agreed-value coverage.
- Make sure your policy covers the real threats to collections — mysterious disappearance, breakage, transit damage, spoilage, and partial loss of pairs and sets.
- Work with specialist carriers for serious collections.

Risk Avoidance

- Some pieces might be safer in professional storage than on display at home, even if you want to keep them in your house.
- Think hard before lending to exhibitions because the exposure may not be worth the prestige. And be careful about publicizing what you own.

Risk Retention

- Accept reasonable deductibles
- Choose to self-insure lower-value pieces that don't justify the cost of appraising them.

Collections are more than investments. They're reflections of your taste, passion, and your history. Losing a piece hurts far beyond its dollar value, and insurance can't fix that. What it can do is keep financial loss from piling onto emotional loss.

Know what you have. Document it. Schedule it. And work with people who understand what you're protecting.

In Chapter 6, we turn to a different kind of exposure—one that has nothing to do with what you own and everything to do with what you might owe. Liability risk scales with wealth in ways that aren't intuitive, and the legal landscape has shifted dramatically in recent years. When a single verdict can exceed $10 million, understanding how to structure your protection isn't optional. It's essential.

Clear and Present Danger

No doubt, by now you've noticed a pattern: your success has made you a target. Not in a paranoid, everyone's-out-to-get-you sense. In a practical, this-is-how-litigation-works sense. When people get hurt, and attorneys get involved, the first question isn't just, "Who's at fault?" It's, "Who can pay?"

While we have touched on liability exposure earlier in this book, this chapter addresses that exposure in far more detail. We look at the litigation landscape you're operating in, the liability coverage you're likely to need, and how to structure protection commensurate with your own situation.

Plaintiff's attorneys in injury suits most often work on a *contingency* basis, meaning that they don't get paid unless they recover money for their clients. So before taking on a case, they evaluate three things: liability (is the defendant at fault?), damages (how badly was the plaintiff hurt?), and collectability (can the defendant pay?).

Visible wealth answers that third question emphatically. You can pay. Everyone knows it. And that knowledge shapes who gets sued, for how much, and how aggressively.

This isn't entirely unfair. The thinking goes that if you cause harm, you should compensate the victim. But it does mean that identical accidents produce different outcomes based on who caused them. A driver with a minimum wage income who causes a serious accident might be sued up to the policy limits of their basic insurance. You, causing the same accident, might face a claim for millions — because the plaintiff's attorney knows there's more to recover. The question is whether you're protected when those claims come?

What's that saying about assumptions?

Robert and Susan were both working professionals who made a fantastic living. Despite a joint personal net worth of around $16 million, they had a bargain-bin auto policy with state-minimum liability limits and no liability umbrella. They had reasoned that setting high liability limits would make them a more attractive target for lawsuits and that keeping limits low would discourage plaintiffs' attorneys from pursuing them.

They had it precisely backwards. Low limits don't discourage lawsuits; they just mean your personal assets are exposed. A plaintiff's attorney sees someone in their position with minimum coverage and thinks "shallow policy, deep pockets". That's not a deterrent. It's an invitation for disaster.

One sunny September afternoon, Susan was driving near her home when she had a momentary lapse in attention. She drifted onto the shoulder and struck a pedestrian, paralyzing him.

Unsurprisingly, the injured man and his attorney declined to settle for the $25,000 offered by the insurance carrier. After all, $25,000 in coverage was pocket change compared to the life-changing injuries sustained. They did, however, sue. After about a year of mediation, they settled for $3 million, which Robert and Susan personally paid. $3 million from assets they'd spent decades building, which could, and should have been covered by a more suitable insurance policy.

These people hadn't thought they were being careless when they chose their policy limits. On the contrary, they were busy and successful, but unfortunately, following a misguided strategy.

This is just one of the gaps — albeit a devastating one — that a good risk advisor looks for.

"shallow policy, deep pockets"

The Litigation Landscape

Even a quick look at the litigation environment will tell you that it has changed dramatically over the past few decades, yet most people's insurance coverage hasn't kept pace.

What once seemed like extraordinary legal outcomes are now routine. *"Nuclear verdicts"*, in which the awards exceed $10 million, regularly make headlines, but even ordinary serious injury cases generate claims in the low millions. Medical expenses alone for catastrophic injuries can reach seven figures. Add lost wages, future care costs, and pain and suffering, and the numbers climb rapidly. Some juries have shown a willingness to award enormous sums, particularly against defendants perceived as wealthy. The psychology is understandable: a plaintiff with life-altering injuries sits in front of a jury, and a defendant who is guilty and who can obviously afford to pay sits across from them.

Empathy flows toward the injured party, and the ensuing verdicts reflect it.

Yet many affluent families still carry umbrella coverage that hasn't kept pace with this reality, operating on outdated assumptions about what constitutes adequate protection.

The Many Ways You Can Be Sued

While by no means a comprehensive list, here are a few of the more common ways that I've seen people become exposed to liability.

Auto accidents are the most common source of liability claims. Every time you or a family member gets behind the wheel, you're creating exposure. An unavoidable mechanical failure, an icy road, or, as in Susan's case, a momentary distraction, and someone could be seriously injured. If you're found to be at fault, you're liable for their damages.

Premises liability claims are also far too common and can occur in or on property you own or control. Let's say a guest slips on your wet deck, a visitor trips on a raised flagstone, or a visiting relative drowns in your pool. If someone is hurt on your property, you may be liable regardless of how careful you were.

Watercraft and recreational vehicle incidents create exposure beyond standard auto and premises liability. Boating accidents, jet ski collisions, and ATV injuries are all frequent reasons for claims, and serious accidents of this type are common.

Professional activities and board service can generate personal liability even when you're acting in a professional capacity. Directors and officers of companies and non-profits can be sued personally for board decisions or omissions — a topic we'll address briefly later in this chapter.

Defamation and personal injury claims arise from perceived harm to a person's reputation or dignity and may include libel, slander, invasion of privacy, and false imprisonment. Often, people are unaware of their exposure to such liability until a claim arrives.

Social host liability can arise whenever you serve alcohol to guests. If you host a party, for example, and serve alcohol to someone who becomes intoxicated, you can be held liable in many states if that person goes on to injure someone on their way home.

Each of these categories represents the potential for claims of significant magnitude. By their nature, most affluent families have exposure across multiple categories simultaneously.

Vicarious Liability: Responsibility for Others' Actions

It may seem counterintuitive, but you're not only responsible for harm you cause directly, you can also be held liable for harm caused by others. However, it's true, and this extends your exposure far beyond your own behavior — no matter how careful you are.

One major source of liability are the actions of your children. For example, if your teenager causes an accident while driving a car you own, you're liable. If your child negligently damages property or injures someone, as their parent, you may be held responsible.

Your sphere of responsibility doesn't stop at your offspring. Consider the people you employ, such as domestic employees, whose actions within the scope of their employment are also your responsibility. That means if your housekeeper injures a visitor while performing her duties, you're liable. Similarly, if your driver causes an accident while on duty, you're liable. This extends to household employees of all types — a topic we cover in more detail in Chapter 7.

Finally, anyone who drives your vehicle can expose you, as the owner, to liability. If you lend your car to a friend and they cause an accident, you can be named in that lawsuit. And if you lend a vehicle to someone you know — or should have known — was an unsafe driver, you could be on the receiving end of a *negligent entrustment* claim.

Vicarious liability means your exposure isn't limited to your own conduct. It extends to everyone in your orbit whose actions could create liability that attaches to you.

Even the most innocuous of circumstances can expose a well-meaning person to unwanted liability. But with advance planning, it doesn't have to result in financial chaos.

No Good Deed Goes Uncovered

Eileen had just settled into her new home after downsizing. Once the unpacking was done, she had several stacks of used moving boxes — still in good shape — that she didn't want to go to waste. She posted them for free in a local Facebook group, and before long, a gentleman messaged saying he'd love to take them off her hands.

The next day, the man, in his early 60s, arrived. He loaded the boxes into his truck and, when he had finished, turned to Eileen and offered to pay her. The boxes were in such good condition, he said, and he felt bad just taking them for free.

Eileen refused. It was her pleasure.

Still wanting to express his gratitude, the man asked if there was anything he could do for her. She thought for a moment. "Actually, I have a few boxes of Christmas decorations that need to go up to the attic. If you wouldn't mind helping me get them up there, I'd be very grateful." She said.

He was happy to help. Grabbing her ladder, he set it up in the garage beneath the attic hatch and started climbing with a box in hand. At the top, as he reoriented the box to fit it through the opening, he lost his balance. The box dropped first, then he swiftly followed. Tumbling from the ladder onto the concrete garage floor, the man hit his head and was unconscious before Eileen could reach him.

She called 911. The paramedics arrived swiftly and rushed the man away. Eileen heard nothing more for about a week.

When the call came, it was from his son. His father was still in the hospital. The fall had caused a brain bleed, so he'd spent four days in a medically induced coma in the ICU. With no health insurance, the bills for his care were mounting, and they weren't sure when — or whether — he'd be able to return to work.

Eileen called me in a panic. She felt terrible for the man and his family, but at the same time was also terrified she might lose her house.

I walked her through the process. I reminded her of the protections that we had put in place for her. I comforted her and reassured her that she would be okay, and we filed a claim under her homeowners policy. Her carrier paid out the medical payments coverage immediately

— $10,000, no questions asked, no liability determination required. Med Pay exists precisely for situations like this: someone is hurt on your property, they need help now, and you want to provide it without delay.

But $10,000 clearly wasn't going to cover an ICU stay and months of lost income. To determine liability, the carrier investigated and found that the garage floor was level and safe— there was no hazard. But the ladder was rickety, not something that should have been used. That was enough to decide that Eileen was liable.

Her insurance ultimately paid the man $450,000, and Eileen was protected from any further action by him or his family.

Here's the thing: we had built Eileen a solid insurance program precisely for unknown dangers like this. Her homeowners policy included $1 million in liability coverage, and she carried a $5 million umbrella on top of it. The $450,000 claim was paid entirely by her carrier. Her assets were untouched and she didn't lose her house.

While $450,000 is a considerable sum, it could have been much worse.

Imagine she'd been carrying inadequate liability coverage. What would have happened to her? And what would have happened to the man? Would he have had to sue her to get his medical care paid for?

Remember that even everyday kindness can expose you to liability you never expected. The right coverage ensures that a generous act doesn't become a financial catastrophe — for you or for the person you were trying to help.

As with all the risks we identify, it makes sense to evaluate it from the perspective of the four pillars. That's where we're going next.

Risk Reduction: Minimizing Liability Before it Arises

Before we discuss how to transfer liability through insurance, it's worth recognizing that some liability exposure can be reduced at source. While you can't eliminate the risk of being sued entirely, you can reduce the likelihood of incidents that will lead to lawsuits — and strengthen your position if claims arise anyway.

Property maintenance is a liability reduction. There are steps you can take on your property to reduce risk before accidents occur. These include adequate lighting on walkways and stairs; slip-resistant surfaces around pools; secure handrails, and trees trimmed so that dead branches aren't waiting for the next windstorm to drop onto a guest's car — or head. These aren't just aesthetic choices or homeowner chores. They're proactive decisions that reduce the probability of someone getting hurt on your property. And if an injury does occur, well-documented maintenance practices strengthen your defense.

Driver selection and training matters enormously. If you have teenage drivers in your household, your auto liability exposure has increased dramatically, not because they're irresponsible, but because they're inexperienced. Statistics don't lie; young drivers are significantly more likely to be involved in serious accidents. This is why professional driver training — not just the minimum required for licensure, but genuine high-quality instruction — is worth far more than it costs. In addition, some families establish driving contracts with their teenage children to set clear expectations about passengers, nighttime driving, phone use, and the consequences of non-adherence. These aren't just parenting tools. They're important methods for reducing risk.

Supervision of high-liability activities makes a difference. When you host a pool party, someone should be watching the pool — not glancing at it occasionally while refreshing drinks. They need to be paying attention. When guests are using your watercraft or recreational vehicles, someone experienced should be present to guide them. And when you're serving alcohol at an event, you should have a fallback plan for guests who've had too much. You don't need to be a helicopter host, but presence and awareness matter.

Screening household employees can reduce vicarious liability exposure. Background checks, reference verification, and proper vetting aren't just about protecting your family and property. They help to ensure that the people whose actions create liability for you are people of sound judgment. The degree of care you take in hiring directly affects your exposure to liability. For this reason, some private client insurers include complimentary background and driving record checks for prospective hires. Check with your risk advisor and see if you have this benefit.

None of this eliminates liability, however. But practicing risk reduction makes incidents less likely and defensible claims more defensible. It's the foundation on which the rest of your liability protection is built.

Risk Transfer: Building Your Liability Protection

For the exposures you can't eliminate — and there will be many — the answer is usually to transfer them. Shift the financial consequences to someone else, primarily through insurance.

Liability transfer is where affluent families are most consistently underprotected. Around the corner may be the accident that wasn't your fault but somehow became your liability, the injury that occurred despite every precaution, or the lawsuit that targets you simply because you're worth targeting.

When those claims come, insurance is what stands between you and financial devastation.

We'll next explore the mechanics of transferring liability, such as umbrella policies, excess coverage, underlying limits, and scope of coverage, to learn how to structure protection to meet your actual exposure. But before we dive into the details, understand this fundamental principle: by obtaining appropriate insurance coverage, you are transferring risk you cannot comfortably bear to carriers who are in the business of bearing exactly that. In return, you pay premiums — a known, manageable cost — to avoid potentially catastrophic, unknown costs. That exchange is the heart of risk transfer.

The question isn't whether to transfer liability risk. It's how much, through what structures, and at what cost.

Understanding Umbrella Coverage

The first weapon in your armory should be an umbrella policy. This sits above your *underlying policies* — auto, homeowners, watercraft, or whatever else you have — and provides extended liability limits for when claims exceed the underlying limits. In Eileen's case, it was what prevented her from financial ruin when faced with a claim.

Here's how it works. Your auto policy might provide $500,000 in liability coverage, but your umbrella might provide an additional \$5 million. If you cause an accident that results in \$3 million in damages, the auto policy would pay the first \$500,000, after which the umbrella would cover the remaining \$2.5 million.

Umbrella vs. Excess Liability Policies

There's a distinction that's worth understanding between umbrella policies and *excess liability policies*, even though you may have heard some in the insurance industry use the terms interchangeably.

An excess liability policy is essentially a deeper bucket of money from which to draw. Helpfully, it uses the same language as you'll find in your underlying policy — same inclusions, same exclusions. If your underlying policy covers a claim, the excess policy extends those limits. Conversely, if your underlying policy doesn't cover a claim, neither does the excess. It can provide more money, but not broader protection.

An umbrella policy, on the other hand, can provide coverage that goes beyond your underlying policies. Defense costs, for example, might be covered outside of limits even when your underlying policy includes defense costs within its limits. There are other helpful features as well. The coverage territory might be broader than your basic policy and may include personal injury liability, such as defamation, invasion of privacy, or false arrest — even when your underlying policies don't include it. This broader coverage distinguishes a true umbrella policy from a pure excess policy.

That said, in practice, carriers typically offer one or the other, not both. So, the type of policy you get is often determined by the carrier you choose. For the remainder of this chapter, we'll use the term "umbrella" to refer to both policy types, as is common in the industry. But it's important you understand that differences exist and may matter depending on your situation and the specific policies available to you.

The Underlying Limits Requirement

A critical point many people miss is that umbrella policies require minimum underlying limits on your auto, homeowners, and other insurance policies.

A typical umbrella policy might require $250,000 per person and $500,000 per accident in auto liability, and $300,000 in homeowners liability before you can obtain the additional coverage. If your underlying limits are below these thresholds, you have a problem.

It's also important to note that the umbrella doesn't simply pick up where your underlying policy ends. It is activated where the required underlying limits would end. If you're required to have $300,000 in underlying coverage but you only carry $100,000, and you receive a $400,000 claim, here's what happens: your underlying policy pays to its limit of $100,000, the umbrella expects $300,000 to have been paid before it kicks in, and you must personally pay the $200,000 shortfall.

This gap exists because you didn't maintain the underlying limits required by the umbrella. It's your responsibility, not the umbrella carrier's, to keep tabs on this.

The best approach is to review your umbrella policy and identify the required underlying limits, then review your auto and homeowners policies to confirm that your actual limits meet or exceed those requirements. If your umbrella requires $500,000 in auto liability and you carry $300,000, you have a gap. Or if your umbrella requires $300,000 in homeowners liability and you carry only $100,000, you also have a gap.

Increasing underlying limits is usually inexpensive and will cost you no more than a few hundred dollars per year. It's a step worth taking, though, because the gap itself can cost hundreds of thousands in an actual claim.

If you have multiple properties across multiple states, especially if you use a different risk advisor in each state due to their geographic limitations, it is critical to double-check that all policies coordinate properly with your umbrella. I have a client who had four different insurance agents in four different states before we connected.

His primary home, autos, and umbrella policies were insured with one agent in Florida, while his secondary homes and auto policies were insured with different agents in Wyoming, California, and Wisconsin. Since I am licensed in all 50 states and D.C., I was able to look at everything holistically for him. Together, we discovered that two of his out-of-state auto policies did not meet the requirements of his umbrella policy, creating a $200,000 gap in each state! That was one of the first things we corrected.

What Umbrellas Cover – And What They Don't

Umbrella policies are broad, but they're not unlimited. Understanding the scope of coverage matters.

What is typically covered:

- bodily injury and property damage liability
- personal injury (defamation, invasion of privacy, or false arrest)
- liability arising from your residence, vehicles, or watercraft
- liability arising from your actions anywhere in the world
- defense costs in addition to limits.

What is typically excluded:

- intentional acts (harm you cause deliberately)
- business activities (you need commercial coverage for that)
- professional liability (errors in professional advice or service)
- employment-related claims (wrongful termination, discrimination)
- criminal acts
- contractual liability (obligations you've assumed by contract)
- pollution liability
- *punitive damages* in some states

When faced with a claim, the exclusions matter. If your umbrella excludes employment-related claims and your nanny sues you for wrongful termination, the umbrella won't respond.

To identify the gaps where you are exposed, review your umbrella's exclusions and understand what's not covered. Where you find excluded categories, you may need other coverage to address them.

How Much Coverage Do You Need?

Let me be direct: $1–2 million in umbrella coverage is not adequate for families with significant wealth.

As we've seen, serious injury claims routinely exceed $5 million, and nuclear verdicts can reach well beyond that. A $2 million umbrella may sound like a lot of money, but it's not a lot of coverage. It might fund the defense of a serious claim but leave nothing for settlement if the total defense costs exceed the policy limit. Or it might cover a moderate claim and leave you personally exposed on a serious one.

So, how much do you need? Every situation is different, but I try to determine umbrella limits based primarily on the value of your tangible, insurable assets — your homes, vehicles, watercraft, and other property. From there, I factor in additional considerations, such as your public profile, earning potential, and overall level of exposure. Variables that push me toward suggesting higher limits might include owning multiple properties, the presence of pools and *attractive nuisances*, teenage drivers in the family, watercraft or ATVs, board positions, significant entertaining, and employing household staff. If several of these apply to you, you should assume that the appropriate coverage is at the higher end of what carriers will offer.

To get a sense of where you stand, a Liability Adequacy Calculator is included in the Appendix of this book. It walks you through the factors that should inform your umbrella limits — net worth, property exposures, vehicles, household staff, public profile, and lifestyle risks — and provides a framework for the conversation with your advisor. A fillable PDF version is also available at www.fortifiedbook.com/resources.

Losing Traction

The Harmons had built a successful shipping logistics business and accumulated a net worth of approximately $8 million. They were prudent, so their approach to financial planning included purchasing adequate insurance and adopting a sensible risk-management program. Their umbrella policy provided $5 million in coverage. At far more than what many of their friends carried, and more than their advisor's typical client, this seemed substantial, and they felt well-protected.

Their 18-year-old son, David, was driving home from college on a rainy evening. He was at the speed limit, being careful. But wet roads are unforgiving. When the car in front of him braked suddenly, David couldn't stop in time. His car hydroplaned, spun, and collided with an oncoming vehicle.

The driver of the other vehicle was a 34-year-old mother of two, who suffered catastrophic injuries. She underwent multiple surgeries and required months of rehabilitation. Even worse, she was left with a permanent disability that ended her career. The financial and emotional devastation for her family was profound. The claim against David — and therefore against his parents, as the vehicle's owners — ultimately settled for $7.5 million.

The auto and umbrella policies paid out in full, a total of $5.25 million. But the additional $2.25 million had to be personally funded by the Harmons. Thankfully, they could pay it and weren't ruined. But the financial architecture of their lives had to be rebuilt around a new, and unexpected, $2.25 million hole.

The lesson: "substantial" coverage isn't the same as adequate coverage. Adequate is relative to your net worth and exposure, not simply what sounds like a big number.

Personal Liability

Coverage	Private Client	Standard Market
Available Excess Limits	Up to $100 Million	Up to $5 Million
Defense Costs	Outside Policy Limits	Inside Policy Limits
Uninsured/Underinsured Motorist	Up to $10 Million	Up to $1 Million
Medical Payments	$10,000	$1,000
Choice of Attorney	Select From Top Firms	Carrier Assigns
Personal Attorney Costs	Up to $100,000 Available	Not Available
Worldwide Travel Protection	Available	Not Available
Nonprofit Board Liability	Up to $1 Million	Not Available
Kidnap, Ransom & Extortion	Available	Not Available

Liability must be measured against the characteristics of your life, and covered accordingly. Note: Coverage features, limits, and availability vary by carrier and state.

Structuring Liability Protection

For families needing coverage beyond the limits of standard umbrella policies, structuring liability protection becomes undeniably more complex. However, this complexity is manageable with the right advisors.

Why Multiple Carriers Are Sometimes Necessary

Individual insurance carriers have capacity limits — they'll only write so much coverage for any single insured. You might engage a carrier willing to write a $10 million umbrella policy, but they can't go up to $25 million.

For very high limits, multiple carriers become necessary. This isn't a problem; it's simply how the market works. Specialty brokers who focus on high-net-worth clients coordinate these placements regularly to great effect.

Legal Entities as a Complement to Insurance

As we saw in Chapter 3, sophisticated asset protection through risk transfer can also involve legal structures that separate risky assets from protected wealth.

There are two main structures that might be useful. The first is an LLC, which can hold property or other assets, thereby separating the liability associated with an asset from its owner's personal wealth.

Alternatively, trusts can hold assets to protect them from creditors, but not all trusts are the same. The first type is a *revocable trust*. These are great for estate planning, but do virtually nothing for asset protection because you are likely still in control of the asset in the trust, by virtue of being the trustee. If you are looking to form a trust to protect the asset, consider an *irrevocable trust*, though they are far more restrictive.

For all LLCs and trusts you use, it is vital to add them as "Additional Insureds" on your relevant policies. This might include your home, umbrella, and auto, if the autos are held in the entity.

These structures complement insurance, not replace it. Insurance handles the claims, while legal structures provide back-up protection if those claims exceed coverage or fall outside covered scenarios. As you can see, it's a complex area, and proper asset protection planning requires legal expertise. There's no substitute for working with attorneys who specialize in this area if your wealth and exposure warrant such sophisticated structures.

Risk Avoidance: When the Exposure Isn't Worth It

For exposures that can't be reduced to a manageable threshold, you may want to consider the risk-avoidance pillar.

This is the pillar that high achievers often resist. You've built your success by taking calculated risks, by saying yes to opportunities and not letting fear dictate your choices. The suggestion that you should avoid something can feel like timidity, even though it is in fact discernment.

Consider the backyard shooting range you were planning to install. You've got the acreage, you enjoy recreational shooting, and building a private range sounds like a great way to practice your aim without the hassle of driving to a facility. Sadly, a home shooting range is among the highest liability features you can add to a residential property. Mishaps involving negligent discharge, ricochet, a guest unfamiliar with firearms handling, or a round that travels farther than expected are very real threats. The injury potential they bear is significant, and the injuries tend to be catastrophic. They also give rise to the kind of claims that generate seven-figure judgments.

Is a private range worth that exposure? Maybe. If you're a serious shooter, if the range is professionally designed with proper berms and backstops, or if you control access carefully and never allow unsupervised use, then the convenience may justify the exposure. But for most families, a backyard range adds liability that's difficult to fully transfer and easy to avoid. Owning the land is wonderful. Building the range is optional.

The same calculation applies to certain exotic pets, and to that zipline your kids saw at a resort and now want installed in the yard. You may well decide that your life is better without the burden of this unnecessary risk.

It even applies to decisions beyond property features. The friend who wants to borrow your exotic car for the weekend because he has an important client to entertain? You are entitled to say no. The neighbor who asks to take your jet ski out? You can also decline that politely. The fleeting social discomfort of saying no is considerably less than the financial and emotional devastation of being named in a lawsuit because you said yes.

Risk avoidance also applies to how you engage with potential conflicts. The online argument you're tempted to wade into. The negative review you want to write about a contractor who wronged you. The public statement about a contentious issue. Each of these creates exposure through defamation claims, reputational damage, and conflicts that escalate beyond what you intended. Sometimes the wise choice is simply not to engage.

The goal is to take the risks that matter to you and decline the ones that don't.

Risk Retention: What You're Still Carrying

Even with excellent coverage that follows the guidance in this chapter, some liability exposure remains yours. Understanding what you're retaining — and retaining it consciously — is therefore the final piece of a sound liability strategy.

You also need to understand that coverage has limits — literally. A $5 million umbrella has a $5 million limit, and a $10 million umbrella has a $10 million limit. Even families with $50 million in layered coverage have a $50 million limit. Theoretically, a catastrophic scenario involving multiple fatalities, egregious circumstances, and a plaintiff-friendly jurisdiction with a runaway jury could exceed even the most substantial coverage.

None of this is a reason for panic. Truly catastrophic judgments exceeding eight figures are rare. But it is a reason for realism because nobody can transfer every dollar of potential liability exposure. At some point, you have no choice but to retain the tail risk — the low-probability, high-severity scenarios that exist at the far end of the distribution curve.

Know what you're carrying. Know why — either because it's uninsurable, because the cost of transferring it would be prohibitive, or because you've deliberately chosen higher deductibles in exchange for lower premiums. And maintain the resources to absorb retained exposure if it materializes.

Special Considerations

Board Service

Serving on boards, whether corporate, nonprofit, or homeowners' association, creates directors and officers liability exposure. In effect, board members can be personally sued for decisions the board makes or fails to make. Many organizations carry directors and officers (D&O) insurance to protect board members, but this coverage may be inadequate, contain gaps, or have been depleted by claims against other board members before your claim is addressed. Also, typical D&O insurance policies have *eroding limits*, meaning defense costs reduce the coverage amount before a judgment is even rendered. Another limitation is that these policies typically don't cover a board member who sues another board member.

Before joining any board, it's prudent to understand what D&O coverage exists and whether you think it's adequate. If coverage is weak or nonexistent, think carefully about whether the exposure is worth the benefits of service. If you decide it is and join the board, speak with your risk advisor to discuss adding D&O coverage to your umbrella.

Choice of Counsel

Do you like your attorney? If you were sued, would you like your attorney involved in your robust defense, or are you satisfied letting your insurance company choose your counsel? Be aware that most standard insurance policies give the insurance company the exclusive right to select counsel on your behalf.

Some private client policies offer the right to select your own defense attorney, or at least to have meaningful input into the selection. This is worth asking about when evaluating carriers. If your current policy doesn't offer this option, discuss it with your risk advisor — it may be available as an endorsement, or it may be reason enough to consider a carrier that provides it. I know that when I am in the defendant's chair, I want Ben Matlock.

The Annual Review

Liability coverage isn't set-and-forget. Your situation changes constantly, meaning that your net worth fluxuates, you acquire new properties or vehicles, add new drivers into the household, assume new board positions, and your public profile might grow. To keep abreast of all these exciting developments, you'll need to build an annual liability review into your risk management process. If anything significant has changed, that is your opportunity to re-evaluate your coverage. What was adequate last year may be insufficient this year.

The Four Pillars Applied to Liability

Risk Reduction

- Maintain properties to minimize injury risk.
- Ensure all household drivers are properly trained.
- Supervise high-liability activities.
- Screen household employees thoroughly.

Risk Transfer

- Carry an umbrella with a coverage limit appropriate to your actual exposure.
- Ensure underlying policies meet umbrella requirements.
- Consider layered excess coverage for significant wealth.
- Verify your umbrella covers your actual exposures (watercraft, recreational vehicles, etc.)

Risk Avoidance

- Evaluate high-liability features against their value to you.
- Decline to lend vehicles or equipment when the exposure isn't worth it.
- Be thoughtful about hosting events where alcohol will be served.

Risk Retention

- Choose deductibles consciously based on your ability to absorb losses.

- Understand your policy exclusions — each represents retained risk.
- Maintain liquidity for deductibles and retained exposure.
- Accept that some exposure is unavoidable.

We've talked a lot about different sources of liability risk in this chapter, but there's one category of liability exposure that deserves a chapter of its own, because it's where affluent families are most consistently underprepared: the people who work in your home.

In Chapter 7, we turn to the household enterprise — the nannies, housekeepers, estate managers, and other domestic employees who make your life run smoothly. They also create legal obligations that most families don't know they have.

7

The Household Enterprise

A few years ago, a colleague of mine shared a story about their client, let's call her Carol.

The Slip-Up

Carol's full-time housekeeper, Alice, had slipped on a wet tile floor while cleaning, badly injuring her back. She was rushed to the hospital, and while there, the hospital learned that Alice was hurt on the job, so they proceeded to help her file a *workers' compensation* claim. This raised a red flag with the state, because Carol didn't carry workers' compensation insurance. Why would she? She'd always viewed Alice as an independent contractor, so she'd never set up a payroll service, issued a *W-2*, or secured any employment-related insurance coverage.

Alice was out of commission for nine weeks but eventually returned to work. In addition to Alice's medical bills and physical therapy, Carol found herself facing fines and penalties from the state for failing to provide workers' comp insurance (a requirement in her state), as well as penalties and back taxes from the IRS for failing to issue W-2s and failing to withhold and pay payroll taxes. After the dust settled, Alice's fall cost Carol close to $200,000.

Carol's situation is far more common than you'd think. And it illustrates something that surprises most of my clients: you're probably an employer too.

Not in the sense of running a business with offices and an HR department, although you may be that as well. I mean, in the closer-to-home sense, having people who work in your home: the housekeeper, the nanny, the gardener, the personal assistant, or the estate manager. Because these people work for you, under your direction and in your space, that makes you an employer with legal responsibilities, potential liabilities, and obligations that a lot of affluent families never think about.

The moment you hire someone to work in your home, whether on a full-time or part-time, live-in or visiting basis, you've stepped into a regulated relationship governed by rules about wages, taxes, workplace injuries, and employee rights.

The Legal Reality of Household Employment

When you think about it, it makes sense that household employers should be subject to the same employment laws as businesses. The same federal laws apply, including the *Fair Labor Standards Act* (FLSA) that governs minimum wage and overtime, and the anti-discrimination statutes that protect workers in every setting. State laws add additional requirements that are often stricter than federal laws, so you would be well advised to ensure you know what applies where you live.

Because household employment law is heavily state-driven, two families with identical staff arrangements can face very different obligations depending solely on where they live. The fact that you may not see yourself as a "real" business doesn't matter. In the eyes of the law, if you control someone's work, you're their employer.

Employee vs. Independent Contractor

The most common mistake homeowners make regarding domestic staff is misclassifying workers as independent contractors when they're actually employees. The distinction matters enormously. For employees, you must withhold and pay employment taxes on their behalf, provide workers' compensation coverage in most states, and comply with wage and working time laws. For a true independent contractor, you pay them and issue a 1099—and that's largely it.

Classification is a legal determination based on the nature of the relationship, not a choice you make for convenience. The core question is control: do you dictate when, where, and how the work is performed? A housekeeper who comes to your home according to your schedule, uses your supplies, and performs tasks you direct is an employee. When viewed through that lens, most household workers are employees by every applicable test.

The consequences of getting this wrong are not trivial. The IRS can impose back taxes, penalties, and interest. State agencies can levy additional fines. And if an injured worker who was misclassified as a contractor files a claim, you'll face the full cost of that injury without the protection that proper classification and insurance would have provided.

Wage, Hour, and Tax Obligations

Once you accept that the people working in your home are employees, a set of concrete obligations follows. You must pay at least the applicable minimum wage, which varies significantly by location. You must pay overtime, though the rules for live-in workers vary by state. And you must keep accurate records of hours worked and wages paid, including compliance with any applicable state meal and rest break requirements.

Then there's the so-called *"nanny tax."* When you pay a household employee more than the annual IRS threshold amount, you must withhold Social Security and Medicare (FICA) taxes, match those contributions with your own, remit the taxes, issue W-2 forms at year's end, and file a *Schedule H* with your personal tax return. It sounds onerous, but it's straightforward once the systems are in place.

Many families ignore these obligations, paying in cash and hoping no one notices. The risks of that approach are very real. If your employee ever files for unemployment or Social Security benefits, the government is immediately alerted that you haven't been paying into the system. And if you're ever nominated for a position requiring Senate confirmation, household employment compliance is standard vetting — a few thousand dollars in unpaid nanny taxes has derailed more than one high-profile appointment.

There's no good reason for non-compliance. Payroll services specializing in household employment handle all of this for a few hundred dollars per year—a modest annual fee that eliminates an entire category of exposure.

Workers' Compensation: Non-Negotiable Coverage

Workers' compensation provides benefits to employees who are injured on the job, covering uncapped medical expenses, rehabilitation, and wage replacement. In exchange, the employee generally gives up the right to sue the employer for those injuries. That trade-off is the heart of the system: assured benefits for the employee, protection from lawsuits for the employer.

State requirements vary dramatically: some require coverage for any household employee, while others exempt small household employers. In New York, for example, coverage is required for all domestic employees who work more than 40 hours per week or are live-in. California currently requires workers' comp insurance for employees who work more than 52 hours or earn more than $100 in a 90-day period. Texas allows employers to opt out entirely, but doing so exposes them to lawsuits without the liability protections that workers' comp provides.

My advice is to carry workers' comp for your household staff regardless of whether your state requires it. The cost is modest, often a few hundred to a couple thousand dollars per year, depending on the number of employees and their roles. Without coverage, you're personally liable for medical bills and lost wages that can easily exceed $100,000 for a serious injury. You also lose the "exclusive remedy" protection that prevents employees from suing beyond workers' comp benefits, and you're likely to face penalties for operating without required coverage. Think back to Carol: a policy costing a few hundred dollars a year would have prevented the entire ordeal.

Employment Practices Liability

Workers' compensation covers physical injuries. But what about claims that you've wronged an employee in other ways —through discrimination, harassment, wrongful termination, or other employment misconduct? That's where employment practices liability (EPL) coverage comes in.

EPL claims against households are more common than most people realize. They include wrongful termination (you let a nanny go and she alleges it was because of her pregnancy or national origin), discrimination (an applicant claims they weren't hired because of race or religion), harassment (a household employee alleges inappropriate comments from a family member), wage and hour disputes (allegations of unpaid overtime or off-the-clock work), or allegations of retaliation after an employee is terminated.

The informal nature of household work increases the risk of these types of claims. Without an HR department, written policies, or consistent documentation, disputes often come down to your word against theirs. That's a precarious position for any employer, and it's one that proper practices and coverage can substantially improve.

Managing Household Employment Risk

The good news is that most household employment risks are manageable with the same practices any well-run business would follow. The difference is that most businesses have HR departments and legal counsel to handle these matters. In your household, you'll need to either build those structures yourself or hire professionals to do so.

Hiring Practices

There is never a good reason to skip a thorough hiring process. Before anyone begins working in your home, you'll want to know about any criminal history, verify their employment background, and check their references. You must verify work authorization with an *I-9 form* for every employee, without exception. Create written job descriptions that clearly define responsibilities, hours, and expectations, and make compensation agreements explicit in a signed offer letter that both parties retain.

If the hiring process feels overwhelming, consider using a household employment agency that handles screening and compliance on your behalf. The better agencies will manage background checks, verify credentials, and ensure all employment paperwork is completed before a new hire's first day. The cost is real, but it buys peace of mind and professional-grade compliance from the outset.

Documentation and Policies

Create an employee handbook, even if it's only a few pages. Cover the essentials: work hours, time off, house rules, how to raise concerns, and what constitutes acceptable behavior in your home. It doesn't need to rival a Fortune 500 company's manual, but it does need to be written and signed by every employee.

Beyond the handbook, document performance issues as they occur and keep a record of any complaints and your responses. Maintain up-to-date personnel files containing offer letters, I-9 and W-4 forms, as well as performance notes. Documentation prevents misunderstandings during employment and provides crucial evidence in disputes. When an employee claims they weren't told about a policy, the signed handbook acknowledgment says otherwise. And if your household includes a manager or estate manager who supervises other staff, make sure that person has at least a basic understanding of employment law—an offhand comment during a termination meeting or a failure to document a complaint can provide the basis for a claim.

Proper Termination

Terminations are where household employment risk is most acute. The combination of close personal relationships, informal management practices, and emotional dynamics makes every termination a potential flash point.

Before acting, document your reasons for the decision. Ensure you can articulate a legitimate, non-discriminatory basis for the termination, and that your documentation supports it. For long-tenured employees or contentious situations, consult an employment attorney before the conversation, not after. Comply with your state's final paycheck requirements, which vary considerably. Handle *COBRA* notices for ongoing healthcare if applicable. Recover any property belonging to you and document what was returned. Provide a brief, factual termination letter. In some cases, it may be worth offering severance in exchange for a release of claims.

Employees Who Drive on Your Behalf

If household employees use their own vehicles for errands, school pickups, or other tasks you've directed, their personal auto insurance is your first line of defense if they're involved in an accident. But their policy may not provide adequate coverage, and a serious accident could quickly exceed their limits. If an employee causes a serious injury while running an errand for you, plaintiffs' attorneys will almost always name you as the employer, regardless of whose car was involved.

Require any employee who drives their own vehicle for household tasks to maintain adequate auto insurance and verify it periodically. Your risk advisor can help you determine appropriate minimum limits. For employees who drive frequently or transport your children, consider whether a household-owned vehicle with proper commercial or employer coverage might be a better approach.

Special Situations

Live-In Employees

Live-in arrangements combine employment and housing into a single relationship, creating intertwined legal considerations that differ from those you'd face with employees who commute. If you provide housing as part of the employment arrangement, its value may need to be included as taxable compensation unless the lodging meets IRS requirements for exclusion—generally, the housing must be on your premises, for your convenience, and a condition of employment. Your tax advisor can help you determine how this applies to your situation.

Privacy is another area that becomes complex when employees live on your property. Both you and your live-in staff need to be able to use the space without feeling intruded upon. Clear boundaries about private areas, guest policies, and off-duty hours should be established in writing before the arrangement begins.

Perhaps the most consequential issue arises when the employment ends. When a live-in employee is terminated, housing naturally ends as well, but depending on your state, the employee may have established tenant rights that require you to follow a formal eviction process. This can create an uncomfortable situation in which a terminated employee continues living in your home for weeks or even months. The best protection is a written agreement established from the outset that explicitly addresses both the employment relationship and the housing arrangement, including what happens to the housing when employment ends.

Temporary Workers and Staffing Agencies

Temporary and seasonal workers create employment obligations even when the relationship is brief. A caterer's assistant hired for a single event, a landscaping crew brought in for a seasonal project, or a temporary nanny covering a vacation can all trigger workers' comp requirements and payroll tax obligations.

One effective way to manage this complexity is to use a staffing agency. The agency handles payroll, taxes, workers' comp, and much of the hiring process. The workers are the agency's employees, not yours, which provides meaningful protection. You should understand, however, that you may still be liable for what happens in your home. Harassment by a family member, for example, creates exposure for you regardless of who technically employs the victim. Agencies cost more than direct hiring, but they meaningfully simplify compliance.

Insurance Coverage for Household Employers

Standard homeowners policies weren't designed for household employment. Your premises liability coverage may respond to some employee injuries, but a standard policy provides no workers' compensation benefits and no EPL coverage. If you employ anyone in your home, you'll need to intentionally build that coverage.

Workers' compensation options include standalone policies, homeowners policy endorsements (available from some carriers in some states), payroll service arrangements that bundle coverage with tax compliance, and state funds for employers who can't obtain private coverage.

EPL options typically include homeowners policy endorsements from private client carriers, the simplest approach for most households; standalone EPL policies for complex operations or multiple employees; and umbrella policies that include EPL coverage, though many umbrella policies exclude employment-related claims, so verify the fit carefully. For most households, an EPL endorsement with limits of $500,000 to $1 million is sufficient.

Private client carriers often offer integrated approaches in which the homeowners policy includes optional workers' comp and EPL endorsements, coordinated with umbrella coverage. For households with significant staff operations, these programs provide simpler administration and reduce the number of coverage gaps that can arise when policies are purchased separately. Your risk advisor can help you determine which approach makes the most sense for your situation.

Domestic Employees

Coverage	Private Client	Standard Market
Employment Practices Liability	Up to $1,000,000	Not Available
Domestic Staff Workers' Comp	Available	Not Available
Staff Background Checks	Available	Not Available
Wage & Hour Defense	Available	Not Available
Third-Party Discrimination Claims	Available	Not Available
Worldwide Coverage for Traveling Staff	Available	Not Available
Immigration Compliance Support	Available	Not Available

Note: Coverage features, limits, and availability vary by carrier and state.

The Human Dimension

Before we turn to the formal risk framework, it's worth pausing on something that makes household employment fundamentally different from any other kind: these people become part of your life. They care for your children, maintain your home, and support your daily existence. Over time, genuine relationships develop. Your housekeeper knows your family's rhythms. Your nanny knows your children's fears and favorites. Your estate manager understands how you like things done in ways that no written manual could capture.

That closeness is a gift, but it also creates a tension. The law doesn't see warmth. It sees an employment relationship with rights and obligations. And when things go wrong—as they invariably can in any employment relationship—the absence of structure can turn a manageable disagreement into a legal nightmare.

None of this means you should treat employees coldly or over-formalize relationships that have developed organically. What it means is that you need appropriate structures—compliance, documentation, coverage—running quietly in the background, protecting everyone when things go wrong, while genuine human relationships flourish day to day. The best household employers I work with manage both: they treat their staff with real care and respect while maintaining the systems and protections that any well-run enterprise requires.

The Four Pillars Applied to Household Employment

Risk Reduction

- Implement thorough hiring practices that include background checks, reference checks, and verification of work authorization.
- Offer competitive compensation and benefits to attract and retain quality staff.
- Create and maintain documentation—including employee handbooks, job descriptions, signed acknowledgments, and performance records—that establishes clear expectations from day one.
- Train household managers on employment law basics so that day-to-day management decisions don't inadvertently create exposure.
- Handle terminations carefully, with documentation and legal review before taking any action.
- Use payroll services to ensure ongoing tax and wage compliance.

Risk Transfer

- Obtain workers' compensation coverage regardless of whether your state requires it.
- Add EPL coverage through an endorsement or standalone policy.
- Verify that your umbrella policy doesn't exclude employment-related claims.
- Understand the contractual allocation of risk between you and a staffing agency.
- Require employees who drive their own vehicles for

household errands to maintain adequate auto insurance and verify their coverage periodically.

Risk Avoidance

- Don't misclassify employees as independent contractors.
- Avoid informal cash payment arrangements that leave no paper trail.
- Don't skip background checks or work authorization verification.
- Avoid employment decisions that could appear discriminatory — document legitimate reasons for all hiring, discipline, and termination decisions.
- Don't let personal relationships override proper employment practices.

Risk Retention

- Accept that some employment friction is inevitable, and not every disagreement requires legal intervention.
- Understand that even with coverage, there may be deductibles or uninsured aspects of a claim.
- Recognize that compliance costs are a permanent part of household employment. The alternative is far more expensive.

Your household is an enterprise, so run it like one. Create the systems and protections that enterprises need, while remembering that the people involved deserve fair treatment, proper protection, and genuine respect.

In Chapter 8, we move from the people in your home to the systems that connect your world. Cyber threats can affect affluent families more so, not because they're famous, but because they're valuable, and the digital landscape changes faster than any single defense can keep up with.

8

The Digital Fortress

By the time you read this chapter, I'm sorry to say, it will already be outdated. The threats, defenses, and specific technologies surrounding cybercrime all evolve faster than any book ever could. As dynamic as developments are, and in fact, because they are so rapid, the four pillars framework applies to cyber risk even more, and the principles remain constant even as the details shift.

Take stock of the devices within arm's reach right now. First, you'll probably see your phone. It knows where you are, where you've been, and listens to you even when you aren't speaking into it. Next, you may catch sight of the smartwatch on your wrist, that monitors your heart rate and all your daily movements. Finally, you glance at your laptop. The browser it runs remembers every site you've visited, every search you've made, and every password you've saved.

Now zoom out a bit. Your home thermostat learns your patterns and knows when you are home or away, your security cameras stream footage to servers you'll never see, and your smart TV listens for voice commands while recommending new content based on your viewing patterns. Don't get me started on what I could learn by talking to your toaster…

This is the landscape of modern life. We've traded privacy for convenience so gradually that most of us never noticed the exchange. Every device, every app, and every "free" service collects data about you that is aggregated and sold many times over. And there's nothing you can do to stop it from being leaked or stolen. For affluent families, this data paints a particularly valuable and personal portrait that details your assets, your habits, and your vulnerabilities. Criminals have noticed. So has artificial intelligence.

AI is accelerating every aspect of cybercrime. For example, voice cloning can replicate your spouse from just a few seconds of audio. You may also have noticed that *phishing* emails no longer arrive riddled with typos. Now they read more like they were written by someone who knows you because AI has analyzed enough data to mimic that familiarity. Deepfake videos have already been used to impersonate executives during video calls to get staff to wire enormous sums of money to clandestine accounts. These tools are becoming cheaper, more accessible, and more convincing every month.

What's at Stake

The implications of cybercrime are far-reaching and can rupture every aspect of your life. Not only is your money at risk, but also your identity, place in society, and your family's security.

Your Money

One of the most immediate cyber threats is financial. If you've ever had funds stolen directly from your accounts or fraudulently transferred to criminals, you'll know that it can be done in seconds.

Wire fraud remains the most devastating and all-encompassing of such crimes. Attackers gain access to a series of email accounts, including your own, your attorney's, and your financial advisor's, before monitoring communications between them. This gives the criminals the inside track on upcoming transactions. When a significant transfer approaches, such as a real estate deal closing, a new investment, or a large purchase, they strike. An email that appears to be from someone you trust then provides "updated" wiring instructions. But the signposted account isn't your attorney's escrow; it's separate and controlled by the criminals. The money moves quickly through multiple transfers, often internationally, and disappears.

Attacks like this have grown more sophisticated. In one common variation, criminals don't just send a fraudulent email; they take over the victim's phone number through a *SIM swap*, so when the bank calls to verify the wire, the fraudster answers and confirms that everything is in order. That's enough to release the money.

Account takeovers work similarly. Criminals use stolen credentials, *social engineering*, or compromised email to gain access to your brokerage or bank account, then transfer the funds before you've noticed anything has changed.

Your Identity

Identity theft extends far beyond a stolen credit card. Criminals who obtain your personal information can open new accounts, or set up new credit cards, new loans, and new lines of credit, all using your identity. Not only this, but they can take over existing accounts by convincing customer service representatives that they're you. And they can file fraudulent tax returns in your name, claiming refunds before you file your own returns. (They're welcome to file mine, so long as they're also willing to pay when I end up owing!)

The financial damage is often recoverable, but the time you'll lose repairing it is not. Victims of Identity theft spend months —sometimes years—disputing fraudulent accounts, correcting credit reports, and proving their identities. It's a grinding, life-disrupting process that can consume hundreds of hours.

And it lingers. Even after the immediate damage is repaired, the ongoing anxiety can be devastating.

Your Responsibility

Data breaches can make you liable for others' information as well as your own.

Most people don't think of themselves as custodians of others' data. But if you serve on non-profit boards, organize community events, or simply keep contacts in ways that include sensitive details, you might carry exposure you hadn't considered.

Consider this scenario: you volunteer for a fundraising event and collect the names, addresses, and credit card numbers of the attendees on your personal tablet. The tablet is subsequently lost or stolen. Suddenly, you're responsible not only for notifying the affected individuals and providing credit monitoring services but also for defending yourself if someone sues.

Your Family and Inner Circle

Cyber risk doesn't respect generational boundaries. A grandparent who falls for a phone scam, a teenager who clicks the wrong link, an employee who connects to your home network — any of these can become the doorway into your digital life. It's up to you to shield these people you know and care about from also being open to harm because of your busy and high-profile life.

Becoming a Harder Target

Short of staying completely off the grid, you can't eliminate cyber risk in today's world, because those cat videos aren't going to watch themselves, am I right? What you can do, though, is make yourself significantly harder to exploit. The practices listed below won't stop every attack, but they can defeat the vast majority.

Verification Protocols

Any request to transfer funds, change account information, or take significant financial action should be verified through an independent channel, regardless of how plausible it seems. Many scammers think nothing of contacting you directly, so here are some essential ways to avert risk:

- If you receive wire instructions by email, call the purported sender at a number you already have — not one provided in the email.
- If someone calls claiming to be from your bank, hang up and call the number on your card.
- If a family member or close associate calls in distress asking for money, use a pre-established code word to confirm their identity.

Make these protocols explicit. Discuss them with your family and communicate them to your advisors, including your attorney, accountant, financial advisor, and real estate agent. When everyone who has access to your financial life knows the rules, social engineering becomes far more difficult.

Email and Link Hygiene

Most attacks begin with email. A link clicked, an attachment opened, credentials entered on a fake login page — all these actions can create the entry points criminals need.

It never hurts to be reminded not to open attachments from unknown senders. (Yes, even from Nigerian princes who need your help. Maybe especially then.) The first step is to verify the sender's actual email address rather than relying on the display name, which can say anything. Hover over any links before clicking to see where they actually lead. When in doubt, navigate directly to websites from your browser rather than following links. Be especially suspicious of unexpected attachments, even from known contacts, because their account may have been compromised.

Authentication and Access

Strong, unique passwords for every account are table stakes. No one can remember hundreds of different passwords for all the platforms and apps we all use daily, which is why password managers exist. As long as you remember one master password, the manager will handle everything else.

Multi-factor authentication adds a second layer of security beyond passwords. Even if someone steals your credentials, they can't access your account without the second factor. Enable it on every account that offers it, especially email and financial accounts.

Not all multi-factor authentication is equal. Hardware security keys provide the strongest protection, followed by authenticator apps. SMS text codes are better than nothing, but are vulnerable to SIM swapping, as described earlier. Where available, consider using passkeys instead. These biometric or device-based login methods eliminate passwords entirely and resist phishing attacks.

Device and Network Security

To secure your data, it's essential to keep your software up to date. Developers patch security vulnerabilities as they are identified, so delaying installation leaves you exposed to attacks. This is why some insurance policies require you to apply updates within a specific timeframe — fail to comply, and a claim could be denied, leaving you exposed to the full extent of a cyber breach.

To ensure continuity, back up your data regularly and perform full backups at least once a month. Then, if ransomware ever locks your files, these backups let you restore them without paying a ransom.

The threats do not stop at your laptop, and you should also secure your home network. Change default router passwords. Use strong encryption. Consider using a separate network for smart home devices so that, if your thermostat is compromised, it doesn't provide a path to your laptop.

Then there is the small matter of who can see into your home. Despite their protective role — or perhaps because of it — security cameras and nanny cams are among the most sensitive devices in your home — and among the most commonly compromised. Default passwords, outdated firmware, and cheap manufacturers with poor security practices create entry points for hackers. Strangers have watched families through their own cameras, learned their routines, and even observed their children. Some have used the footage for extortion, and others have spoken through camera speakers to terrorize homeowners.

When installing any camera, immediately change the default credentials and keep all firmware up to date. As these devices will have privileged access to the most sensitive aspects of your life, only buy them from reputable manufacturers who prioritize security, even if they cost more. Perhaps even consider whether cameras need internet connectivity at all? Local recording without cloud access eliminates remote hacking entirely, but it sacrifices the convenience of remote viewing. If you have cameras in sensitive areas, such as nurseries, bedrooms, and other private spaces, the trade-off between convenience and exposure deserves serious thought. The security camera you installed can become the vulnerability that defeats it.

Lastly, never modify your devices. "Jailbreaking" a phone or altering factory software voids most cyber coverage and creates vulnerabilities the manufacturer didn't intend.

Training Your Household

Your household's security depends on its least cautious member. Help everyone by establishing clear, easy-to-follow guidelines for handling digital threats.

Children click without thinking, share without considering the consequences, and may not recognize manipulation. As a parent or guardian, having age-appropriate conversations with them about online safety, therefore, really matters — not to frighten them, but to build better habits.

Elderly parents are also prime targets for specific scams. On hearing that their grandchild might be in trouble, that someone is calling to offer tech support, or that the IRS is threatening arrest, even smart people can be fooled. If those people have access to significant assets, or if their compromised information can be used to target you, their vulnerability is yours. The answer is to have regular direct conversations about common scams. Make yourself the person they call before taking action.

It's not only relations that can pose a risk. Household staff with network access or knowledge of family patterns also create exposure, so implement clear policies about technology use, appropriate access limitations, and the same verification protocols that apply to everyone else.

The Advisors Who Hold Your Keys

Your security is only as strong as your weakest advisor.

If your attorney's email is compromised, for example, criminals can intercept communications and insert themselves into your transactions. The risk extends beyond your own devices — it applies to every professional service provider you employ, and every computer, phone, or platform they use.

Ask your advisors about their security practices. Do they use multi-factor authentication? Do they carry cyber coverage that protects their work and their clients? How do they verify sensitive requests? You don't need to audit their systems, but you should feel confident that security is a priority for them.

Cyber Insurance

In this fast-evolving market, personal *cyber insurance* is relatively new, and carriers must continually adjust their policies to address new threats. They constantly face new forms of AI-enabled attacks, social engineering, and emerging technologies. Inevitably, there's a lag. Changes to insurance policies typically require regulatory approval, and that process moves slowly. The worrying trend you read about today may not be addressed in policy language for months or years.

This means cyber coverage is rarely as current as the threats it's designed to address. It would therefore be risky to assume your policy covers every new threat. All the more reason to review your coverage periodically with your advisor and remember that prevention remains your first line of defense.

What Coverage Typically Provides

Personal cyber policies usually include protection for:

Financial fraud losses. These include funds stolen through wire fraud, social engineering, account takeover, or unauthorized transfers — after banks or financial institutions have exhausted their reimbursement funds.

Ransomware and cyber extortion. For situations where you are required to pay for ransom demands (including cryptocurrency), negotiation costs, and professional response services. Many carriers also provide expert consultation to help you respond to such threats.

System restoration and data recovery. This extends to costs incurred to remove malicious code, reinstall software, and recover corrupted or deleted data from your devices.

Identity theft restoration. For victims of identity theft, policies should include provisions for engaging professional services to help restore their credit, dispute fraudulent accounts, and repair the damage. Some policies also cover lost wages and expenses incurred while resolving the theft.

Breach notification costs. If you inadvertently expose someone else's personal information — say, by losing a device containing donor records from volunteer work—this coverage typically helps with investigations, notifications, and credit monitoring for affected individuals.

Privacy and security liability. If someone sues you for failing to protect their personal information, this will cover any defense costs incurred and damages awarded.

What Coverage Requires

To be valid, policies generally require you to maintain reasonable security practices, such as installing up-to-date antivirus software, applying timely updates, and conducting regular backups. Most also require you to report incidents within 30 to 60 days, file a police report for fraud or extortion claims, and get carrier approval before paying ransoms or hiring outside experts.

What Coverage Excludes

Personal cyber coverage is, by definition, for exposures that affect you personally. Any business activities — even a side venture run from your home — usually require separate commercial coverage.

Importantly, events you knew about before the policy started aren't covered, so there is no point initiating a policy for a ransom demand after the fact. Also, this coverage is typically offered on an excess basis, meaning that if your bank or credit card company makes you whole, the cyber policy doesn't double-pay.

Limits and Structure

Coverage limits typically range from $100,000 to $2 million, with sub-limits for specific coverages, such as data recovery or breach notification. Deductibles are usually modest — often $500 or so per incident.

Many high-value homeowners policies now offer cyber coverage as an endorsement, with standalone policies also available for broader protection or higher limits. Either way, the coverage should coordinate with your overall insurance program to avoid inadvertent gaps developing.

Questions to Ask Your Advisor

- What security practices does the policy require me to maintain?
- What's covered if I accidentally expose someone else's personal data?
- Does this include identity theft restoration services?
- What are the limits and sub-limits, and are they adequate for my exposure?
- How does this coordinate with my homeowners policy?

What You Shouldn't Do

Some exposures are best handled by not inviting them in, in the first place. Let's look at some of the risks you can avoid:

Digital behaviors to avoid. It's advisable not to store sensitive information on shared or collaborative platforms where access controls are unclear. If you think your team or advisors can see details that should be private, move them out of shared drives, documents, or software. Also, don't use personal devices for business activities because this creates coverage gaps and blurs the line between personal and commercial exposure. Finally, you should not access financial accounts on public Wi-Fi networks without a VPN.

The air gap concept. Not everything needs to be accessible from everywhere. Some families maintain accounts that are deliberately less well-connected, meaning they are accessible only in person or require multiple verification steps that can't be completed remotely. Sure, it's less convenient. That's the point. The trade-off between convenience and security is real, and sometimes security should win.

Requests to decline. Pressure and urgency are hallmarks of fraud. A legitimate attorney won't mind you calling to verify wiring instructions. Nor will a real bank threaten you for hanging up and calling them back. Anyone who insists you act immediately, without verification, is almost certainly not who they claim to be, and you should view their demands with suspicion.

What You May Have to Accept

Some cyber risk is unavoidable. For the reasons stated earlier about the pace of change and the scale of the risk, perfect security doesn't exist. Pursuing it would mean disconnecting from the digital systems that make modern life function.

The irreducible minimum. Certain things are essential for a busy life in the modern world. The following statements are almost definitely true:

- You will have devices that connect to the internet.
- You will communicate electronically.
- You will conduct financial transactions through digital channels.

What insurance doesn't cover. Even comprehensive cyber coverage has limits that you should know from the outset. The time you spend responding to incidents, the stress of being victimized, the reputational damage that can't be quantified, or the emotional toll of violation — these are yours to bear regardless of what insurance pays after an incident.

Reserves and planning. Deductibles are typically small, but coverage limits cap your protection. Remember that losses above those limits are self-insured, so you will need to maintain liquidity for uninsured losses and recognize that the true cost of a cyber incident extends beyond what any policy can reimburse.

When It Happens

Despite the best precautions, incidents happen. Knowing how to respond limits the damage.

Wire fraud. Time is critical. If you suspect this has happened to you, contact your bank immediately — within hours if possible. Wire transfers can sometimes be recalled if caught quickly, but the window is narrow. Once funds have moved through multiple accounts or been converted into cryptocurrency, recovery becomes unlikely. File a police report. Report the incident to the FBI's Internet Crime Complaint Center (IC3). Contact your cyber insurance carrier. Document everything.

Account compromise. If you have lost control of an account or suspect someone else can access it, change your password immediately — and not just for the compromised account. If you've reused that password elsewhere, change it everywhere. It's best to use a different password for each account and not reuse them. You'll also need to review email forwarding rules and connected applications as criminals often set up persistence mechanisms that survive a password change. To counter this, enable or strengthen multi-factor authentication and review recent activity for unauthorized access or transactions.

Ransomware. This may sound like a broken record, but your first action, if you are subject to ransom demands, should be to contact your cyber insurance carrier. Carriers often provide negotiators and technical resources to help in these situations. It's also crucial that you report the incident to law enforcement. Do not assume paying guarantees recovery. These are criminals you are dealing with, and sometimes the decryption keys they provide don't work. Even worse, paying marks you as someone willing to pay again.

Identity theft. Before doing anything else, place fraud alerts with the major credit bureaus — Equifax, Experian, and TransUnion. Also, consider implementing a credit freeze, which prevents new credit from being opened in your name. You'll then need to review the credit reports produced by all three bureaus for accounts you don't recognize. And you must file an identity theft report at IdentityTheft.gov. Finally, contact your cyber insurance carrier if your policy includes identity theft restoration services.

Prepare for a marathon. The effects of identity theft can persist for years. Like mushrooms, fraudulent accounts you thought were closed might suddenly reappear. Collection calls for debts you didn't incur land in your inbox. Or applications you make for accounts or credit are denied because of damage you thought had been repaired. Professional restoration services—often included with cyber coverage — can handle much of the burden, but the vigilance you require is ongoing.

Building Digital Resilience

What's clear is that the threats we've covered in this chapter will evolve. New attack vectors will emerge. AI will make social engineering more convincing and harder to detect. Even the specific advice in this chapter on passwords and multi-factor authentication may eventually give way to entirely new security paradigms. But the underlying principles will remain.

Reduce your exposure to harm from digital platforms and devices through consistent practices — verification protocols, authentication discipline, family training, and vendor awareness. Alongside that, you can transfer the risks you can't eliminate through comprehensive insurance. Avoid unnecessary exposures by thinking before you click, share, or connect. Finally, we must accept that some risk is inherent to the online environment, so we must build the resilience to recover when prevention fails.

No shield is perfect. But a well-constructed defensive wall buys you time, deters opportunists, and ensures that when something does go wrong, it's a setback rather than a disaster.

The Four Pillars Applied to Cyber Risk

Risk Reduction

- Establish verification protocols for all fund transfers and significant financial actions, and ask your significant others to apply them as well.
- Use a password manager with strong, unique passwords for every account.
- Enable multi-factor authentication on all accounts, especially email and financial.
- Keep all devices and software updated.

- Maintain regular back-ups of important data.
- Secure your home network with strong passwords and encryption.
- Optimize security for cameras and nanny cams — change default passwords, update firmware, and consider local-only recording for sensitive areas.
- Train all household members — children, elderly parents, staff — on cyber threats.
- Ask advisors about their security practices.

Risk Transfer

- Review your homeowners policy for cyber coverage or endorsement options.
- Consider standalone cyber coverage if your homeowners policy is inadequate.
- Ensure coverage includes wire fraud, ransomware, identity theft restoration, and breach notification.
- Verify that coverage limits are appropriate for your exposure.
- Understand what security practices the policy requires to be valid.

Risk Avoidance

- Don't store sensitive information on shared platforms with unclear access controls.
- Don't use personal devices for business activities.
- Don't access financial accounts on public Wi-Fi without a VPN.
- Don't click links or open attachments from unknown senders.
- Don't respond to urgent requests without independent verification.

- Don't modify devices by jailbreaking or altering factory software.

Risk Retention

- Accept that some cyber risk is unavoidable in today's connected life.
- Understand your coverage limits and maintain liquidity for losses that rise above those limits.
- Recognize that time, stress, and emotional toll fall outside what insurance covers.
- Focus on resilience — the ability to recover — rather than perfect prevention.

In Chapter 9, we focus on protecting what extends beyond you — your family, legacy, and the structures that preserve wealth across generations.

9

Succession

For most of this book, we've focused on protecting what you have. After all, you've worked hard to build it. But there's another question worth asking yourself: what happens to all of this when you're no longer here?

It's the natural evolution of success. Over the years, you've accumulated wealth and protected it. It's natural to want it to matter beyond your lifetime — to benefit your children, grandchildren, and the causes you care about.

This shift in your thinking adds a deeper layer to risk management. You're no longer just protecting assets. You're protecting a legacy. Instead of just years, the timeline extends to decades — maybe generations. And the complexity multiplies because families are complicated. Blended families, ex-spouses, stepchildren, family members with special needs, relatives who can't be trusted with money, estrangements — most of us are dealing with at least one of these. Legacy planning must account for all of it.

Remember how the four-pillar model gives us tools to navigate risk? When we talk about what happens after you're gone, most people instinctively gravitate to the same pillar… avoidance. Not Risk avoidance, I mean actual avoidance-avoidance because they don't like talking about it. But, actually, Risk Avoidance is not the worst instinct. Legal structures, trusts, and prenuptial agreements — these are all ways of sidestepping predictable problems before they arise.

But avoidance isn't the only useful pillar here. Risk transfer also plays a huge role, offering ways to use life insurance to provide estate liquidity or umbrella coverage that will protect your heirs' inheritance. Beyond that, risk reduction works in some interesting ways when it comes to family. Preparing your heirs to inherit, building governance structures, and having uncomfortable conversations while you still can, all reduce the risk that unprepared heirs might go on to make decisions that could undo everything you've built. First, let's start with some uncomfortable truths.

Family and Legacy

There's an unpleasant phenomenon of wealth transfer that you've probably heard about. It's that most family wealth doesn't generally survive three generations. The reasons are rarely about investment performance or any economic failure, they're human. Admittedly, wealth dilutes when passed down to multiple descendants, that's just the nature of the beast. But family conflicts and heirs who are unprepared for responsibility and whose values don't include stewardship of wealth are other factors that can contribute to the dwindling of hard-earned estates. Families that stay unified beat the odds. Families that fragment quickly fail faster.

All the legal structures in the world can't prevent heirs from making catastrophic choices. Having a serious chance of preserving wealth requires preparation — and preparation is its own form of risk management.

Pause a moment to think about the risks you face with your property, your wealth, and the things you might be liable for. Overall, you can quantify them, model them, and insure against them. Human risk, however, doesn't work that way. Immaturity, incapacity, entitlement, addiction, bad judgment, toxic relationships — you name it — are all risks that can't be transferred to an insurance carrier. They must be managed differently. Here are some of the key danger areas to watch out for:

Concentration risk in people. Many affluent families are run by a single decision-maker. In other words, everything flows through mom or dad. That works until it doesn't. What happens when that person is suddenly gone? Or gradually loses capacity? If no one else understands how the pieces fit together, the family is exposed in ways no insurance policy could ever cover.

Transition is the highest-risk moment. Death, disability, divorce, and remarriage are the moments when families can fracture. Not because of the events themselves, as bad as they are, but because of what they reveal: many families are fractured by unclear lines of authority, competing interests, unspoken resentments, or heirs who aren't ready to assume responsibility. Succession transitions can break families more often than physical losses do.

Compounding probability over time. You have a one percent annual probability of experiencing a significant property claim in the US, which may seem acceptably remote. You would take those odds. But over 30 years, that compounds to roughly a 26 percent chance. Over 60 years — your grandchildren's timeline — it hits 45 percent. What seems unlikely in any given year becomes disturbingly probable given enough time. And that's just for property losses. Add in liability claims, and the odds that someone in your family will experience a significant loss become more likely than not.

The Heir Apparent

The Larsons learned this the hard way. They'd done extensive estate planning focused on Sean and Eleanor's eventual deaths. At 42, their son, Lance, was heir to the family business, and over time, he'd worked his way to owning a 30 percent stake. But nobody planned for Lance to die first. What they discovered was that, with coverage worth $500,000 for a man with three children, a large mortgage, and a wife who'd scaled back her career to support his and raise the kids, Lance's life insurance was inadequate. Upon his death, his 30 percent stake in the family business passed to his widow, Renée, who needed liquidity, not illiquid ownership. Renee chose to sell Lance's stake to outside investors, who offered more than Sean and Eleanor could justify paying to buy her out. Having worked so hard for years, Lance's parents wanted to keep the business in the family. Despite having always gotten along, the conflict between the in-laws turned bitter. This could have ended so differently. Lance should have had more life insurance. The business should have had a *buy-sell agreement*. The family should have discussed what happens if someone dies unexpectedly. These conversations didn't happen because everyone assumed they had time.

This reminds us never to put off difficult conversations, because everything you have worked for and future generations' security are at stake.

Governance Before Wealth Transfer

Most estate plans focus on instruments such as wills, trusts, and powers of attorney. Rightly so. These are essential.

But they're not sufficient on their own. They provide structure without context. A trust can specify who receives what and when, but it can't explain why. It can grant authority, but it can't create understanding.

When the person who understood the full picture is gone, families are often left with legally sound instruments, but no shared framework for using them. That's when confusion, conflict, and unintended outcomes begin.

This is where governance comes in. If you're already working with a family office, governance is likely baked into its operations. This means facilitating family meetings, coordinating activities and decisions across generations, and helping to navigate the human side of wealth. But if you prefer to handle things yourself, there are some things you will need to consider:

Governance doesn't have to be elaborate. At its simplest, it means regular family conversations about financial matters. Questions to ask include: What's the current situation? What's coming up? What decisions need to be made? What are the expectations?

The meeting itself matters less than the habit. The benefit of regular communication is that it prevents surprises. It establishes that money is something the family discusses openly. And it gives heirs practice in thinking about these issues before they become responsible for them.

Beyond simply having conversations, consider implementing:

Decision rights versus consultation rights. Who makes decisions, and who gets consulted before they are made? Clarity from the outset might help to prevent resentment later.

Conflict resolution mechanisms. How will disagreements between family members be handled? Mediation requirements, defined processes, and pre-agreed decision trees all work better when they are established before anyone has become angry.

Organized records. A document that lists all accounts, policies, contacts, and key information held by the family's main decision-maker has the power to transform a months-long treasure hunt with executors into a straightforward process after you're gone. As George Bluth Sr. said in Arrested Development, "there's always money in the banana stand" — but only if someone knows to look there.

Advisor relationships. Introduce your key advisors to your family members. They should know and be comfortable with your attorney, accountant, insurance professional, and wealth manager before a crisis requires it. People accept guidance more readily from someone they've met and trust, rather than from a stranger.

Preparing Heirs

Financial literacy isn't the same as financial maturity. Your children might understand how money works without understanding how to make the best financial decisions. That's why it's important to explain to your family why you have chosen certain advisors, how you evaluate risk, and what trade-offs you're willing to make and why.

Remember that smart kids are still capable of making catastrophic choices. If your heirs don't understand insurance, they are likely to make poor coverage decisions. If they don't understand liability, they could take risks that jeopardize the wealth you've given them. And if your heirs don't understand investing, they might fall prey to bad advice and worse advisors.

But financial knowledge isn't the whole picture. The families that preserve wealth across generations don't just teach their children how money works — they pass down the values that guide how it's used. Generosity, stewardship, discipline — but also a sense of what the family stands for. Some families rally around philanthropy. Others around faith, or entrepreneurship, or preserving something they've built together. When heirs share a sense of purpose, wealth becomes a tool for something larger than personal spending. When they don't, it's just money — and money alone rarely survives the third generation.

A Tale of Two Families

Consider these two illustrations and ask which one best reflects you and your family:

Prepared

Larry and Catherine made an important decision early in their marriage: money would not be a taboo subject. When their three children were young, they explained in simple terms why the family made certain choices. They told them why they drove reliable cars instead of flashy ones, why they gave to charity, and why some things were worth spending on while others weren't. As the children grew, so did the conversations. In high school, Larry brought them into discussions about college costs and what trade-offs they might need to make. By their early 20s, the three children had begun to attend annual family financial meetings — not as observers but as participants, actively asking questions and learning how the pieces fit together. At the age of 25, each child received control of a $100,000 trust with little oversight.

Larry and Catherine never called it a test, but that's what it was. Two of the three invested thoughtfully and withdrew only modest sums over time. The third, on the other hand, spent freely — splurging on a sporty car, an extravagant trip abroad, and generous loans to friends that were never repaid. Within three years, that trust had nearly been depleted. Larry and Catherine didn't lecture or punish their child. They simply adjusted the terms of their larger inheritance to include mandatory professional oversight while they continued to learn how to use money responsibly.

When Larry and Catherine died unexpectedly in a car accident a few years later, of course, their children grieved deeply. But they didn't flounder. They knew the estate attorney's name and had already met him. They understood why the trusts were structured as they were. And they knew their parents' intentions because Larry and Catherine had told them what they were, repeatedly, for as long as they could remember. For this family at least, there was no fighting and confusion. The transition was painful, but orderly.

Unprepared

Kathryn had struggled with addiction since adolescence. Her parents, Michael and Hope, loved her fiercely and always believed she would recover. So,

when advisors suggested setting up a trust with professional management for Kathryn, they resisted. It felt
like giving up on her. After they both died, Kathryn and
her siblings each received an inheritance of $8 million
outright. Within a year, she had a charming new
boyfriend who indulged and exacerbated her drug
habit. To onlookers, he was mainly interested in her
money and certainly didn't have her best interests at
heart. They were right, as within two years, she'd
invested $1.5 million in his business venture — a
venture that existed mostly on paper. Not only that, but
she bought a house she couldn't afford to maintain,
hired staff she didn't need, and funded an unsustainable
lifestyle. Within five years, nearly all of her money was
gone. A professionally managed trust could have
provided for Kathryn for the rest of her life. Instead,
she ended up with nothing, relying on siblings for
support, which they provided begrudgingly.

The starkly different outcomes of these stories show that when
planning for the disbursement of your estate, a lot depends on
the individual characteristics of your heirs and how you
prepare for that.

Insurance as a Legacy Tool

It may not be the first thought that comes to mind when
considering how to transfer wealth to the next generation, but
life insurance is often the most efficient way to do so. It creates
certainty where other assets are uncertain, provides liquidity
when estates need cash, and solves problems that other tools
can't. We explore some of the advantages below:

Estate liquidity. When estates owe taxes, payments are due in cash within months. Without liquidity, families may have to sell assets — often at unfavorable prices and often reluctantly. But if appropriate life insurance is in place, it can provide the funds to pay taxes without liquidating the business, the real estate, or the investments that took decades to build.

Inheritance equalization. When it's decided that one child will take over the family business and the others won't, how do you treat everyone fairly? The business may represent most of the estate's value. In such cases, life insurance can provide equivalent inheritances for children who aren't involved in the family business, reducing conflict and ensuring equitable treatment.

Family business succession. Setting up *key person insurance* for your business should provide the capital needed to stabilize the business during death-related leadership transitions. Having buy-sell agreements in place, funded by life insurance, ensures that ownership of the enterprise transfers smoothly and that your family receives fair value.

And don't forget: your liability coverage protects your legacy too. The lawsuit that wipes out your assets also wipes out your children's inheritance, so don't let that happen to you. The umbrella limits applied in your policy should reflect your current net worth, not what it was 20 years ago.

How Structures Protect

The right legal structures can protect against predictable problems, so you should absolutely be having this conversation with your estate attorney as well as your insurance provider. It's important, then, that I share a couple of tips on how to apply pillar-thinking to the structures that you create:

Divorce protection. Assets held in a properly structured trust for your married son or daughter aren't considered part of their marital property. If he or she divorces, the trust assets remain protected. Conversely, outright inheritances that get commingled with marital assets lose that protection and could be claimed by the ex-spouse. *This is risk avoidance — it is a way to structure the inheritance to side-step a predictable threat.*

Prenuptial agreements. Many people worry about the message these might send but remember that they aren't about distrust — they're about clarity. When adult children marry, entering into prenuptial agreements can protect family wealth regardless of what happens to the marriage later. It's wise to normalize these conversations before your children are engaged, because waiting until a wedding is imminent can create conflict. *These offer another form of risk avoidance — addressing the risk before it materializes.*

Spendthrift provisions. If you have concerns over the way money might be spent without your oversight, writing these provisions into a trust can prevent heirs from accessing the principal investment directly. They can also stop creditors from reaching trust assets in the event of a loan default. An heir with a judgment against them, a gambling problem, or poor financial habits can't dissipate what they can't access. *Once again, this is risk avoidance — the effect is to remove the exposure entirely.*

Professional trustees. Family members serving as trustees often face pressure from beneficiaries — pressure that professional trustees are trained to resist. There are emotional ties that make it very hard to be dispassionate when difficult decisions are needed, so it pays to appoint professionals to manage this process. *This is a risk reduction strategy — you can't eliminate family dynamics, but you can reduce their impact on decision-making.*

Discretionary trusts. Rather than simply assigning fixed distributions from the investment, these trusts allow trustees to adjust payouts based on the circumstances. For example, an heir going through a difficult period might receive less, whereas an heir demonstrating responsibility may receive more to reflect their capacity at the time. The structure is designed to adapt to reality. *This is a risk reduction method through flexibility — building in the ability to respond to changing circumstances.*

Special needs trusts. For family members with disabilities, this kind of trust can provide supplemental support without disqualifying them from any government benefits they might need. Life insurance often funds these trusts, converting premium payments into capital for lifetime care, so your attorney will need to work with your insurance provider to set up the arrangement. *This strategy combines risk avoidance (protecting eligibility for benefits) and transfer (using life insurance to fund long-term care).*

Powers of attorney. Assuming they can be established while capacity exists, these allow trusted people to manage a person's affairs if cognitive decline occurs. The time to create them is now — not during a crisis when capacity may already be in question, because by then it is too late. *This is another risk avoidance approach — putting the structure in place before incapacity makes it complicated or impossible.*

Keeping Your Plan Current

Throughout this book, we've talked about how your insurance coverage should evolve as your life changes. The same principle applies to your estate plan — perhaps even more urgently. A will or trust drafted 10 years ago may no longer reflect your family's reality. A new grandchild, a child's divorce, a change in business structure, a shift in tax law — any of these can make existing documents inadequate or even counterproductive. Make it a habit to revisit your estate documents with your attorney every few years, and always after major life events. Coordinate those reviews with your insurance professional and wealth manager. *The structures that protect your legacy only work if they stay current with the life they're designed to protect.*

What Structures Can't Solve

As we learned in Chapter 2, some legacy risks can't be transferred, avoided, or reduced. They have to be retained. Some of the fundamental issues facing all families are as follows:

Family dynamics. No structure can eliminate conflict completely. Siblings who don't get along won't suddenly find harmony because a trust document tells them to. If they resent each other, they will find ways to fight regardless of how carefully you've planned ahead. Yes, you can use structures to reduce friction and provide mechanisms for resolving it, but they can't fix the underlying relationships.

The cost of too much preparation. As in the story of Larry and Catherine, giving heirs responsibility in stages means accepting that some may make mistakes early on. A child who mishandles a $100,000 distribution has learned an expensive lesson. But that lesson, learned early with limited amounts, may prevent them from making far bigger mistakes later. There is a danger in doing too much for your children. Overprotection produces heirs who might never develop the capability to run their own lives.

The Real Question

Legacy isn't what you leave behind. It's what you set in motion. Families that succeed across generations share common traits. They communicate openly about money, prepare their heirs gradually rather than all at once, and build structures that protect against the kinds of predictable problems we've looked at in this chapter. Once all that is done, they accept that some risk is inherent in passing wealth forward — and they plan for it anyway.

The wealth you have painstakingly built can, if sensitively protected in your lifetime, provide for future generations, support family members who need protection, fund causes you believe in, and give children and grandchildren not just money but the wisdom to use it well. What happens when you're not here to decide? Who understands the *why*, not just the *what*? Can your family function without you?

Those are the questions that matter.

The Four Pillars Applied to Family and Legacy

Risk Reduction

- Avoid being dependent on a single decision-maker.
- Make sure your heirs are prepared to take on the responsibility.
- Discuss authority and values to avoid ambiguity.
- Establish regular family meetings as a habit.
- Create conflict resolution mechanisms before emotions run high.
- Clarify decision rights versus consultation rights.
- Test heirs with graduated responsibility before larger transfers.
- Maintain organized records.
- Introduce the key advisors to your family before any transitions are required.

- Review your estate plan with your advisory team every few years and after every major life event.

Risk Transfer

- Ensure you have life insurance to provide estate liquidity and equalize inheritances.
- Check that your umbrella coverage reflects your current net worth.
- Obtain key person insurance and fund buy-sell agreements for family businesses to smooth transitions.
- Implement governance structures that will outlive you.

Risk Avoidance

- Break down any silence around money and power.
- Have the conversation now about unforeseen deaths in the family.
- Use trusts to protect inheritances from divorce to avoid commingling inherited assets with marital property.
- Normalize conversations about prenuptial agreements early, not when a wedding is imminent.
- Consider enlisting professional trustees for heirs who aren't ready to receive direct access to their money.
- Establish special needs trusts and powers of attorney while you are of sound mind.
- Write spendthrift provisions into trusts where the evidence suggests these could protect your heirs from their own worst instincts.

Risk Retention

- Accept that family dynamics create risks that even the best structure can't eliminate.
- Accept that preparing heirs in advance means some will make mistakes along the way — and that's part of the process.
- Recognize that improbable events become far more probable across generations.
- Acknowledge that legacy planning is ongoing — not a one-time event.

In Chapter 10, we step beyond borders. When your life spans multiple jurisdictions — second homes abroad, international travel, business in multiple countries — risk management becomes considerably more complex.

10

Life Abroad

Everything we've discussed in this book so far has assumed the relative simplicity of managing a risk portfolio in one country, with one legal system, and one set of rules. Specifically, the US.

But what happens when life becomes international?

Maybe you own a vacation home in another country—a villa in Italy, a flat in London, or a place on the beach in Mexico? Perhaps your business has grown to include international operations, or you travel abroad frequently for work.

When your life spans international borders, risk management becomes considerably more complex. This is because insurance policies have territorial limits, and liability rules vary dramatically across countries. Not only that, but healthcare systems work very differently, and the legal protections you take for granted at home may not exist abroad. The assumptions underlying every facet of your life shift when geography enters the equation.

This chapter won't make you an expert in international risk management, but it can alert you to the key issues, help you ask the right questions, and ensure you're not inadvertently creating gaps in protection when your life crosses borders.

Two Very Different Risk Profiles

International exposure comes in two fundamentally different forms and conflating them leads to gaps in insurance coverage. It's best to have a clear understanding of the limits of each type.

Temporary exposure includes international travel for business or tourism, extended stays, chartering a yacht abroad, or cruising in foreign waters. Anything where you're simply a visitor. In these cases, your life remains anchored in the US, and your time abroad is measured in days or weeks. The risks are real but episodic, with medical emergencies, accidents, and security incidents among the most consequential. Travel insurance and the international reach of your domestic policies can effectively address most of them.

Permanent or semi-permanent exposure to other countries is a different matter. Owning foreign property, keeping a boat year-round in Mediterranean waters, or spending enough time in another country to raise residency questions will inevitably create ongoing obligations and exposures that temporary solutions can't address. If your life involves these things, you will need local coverage, local compliance, and local expertise. You're no longer visiting; you're operating in another jurisdiction.

The vacation home you use for two weeks each summer sits somewhere between these categories. While it may be temporary in your mind, its exposure is permanent. We'll look at what all this means in practice later in this chapter.

What Follows You Abroad—And What Doesn't

Before leaving the country, it's vital that you understand which insurance coverage travel with you and which will stop abruptly at the border. The pattern, with only a few exceptions, is that less follows you than you might assume. Here are some important areas to be aware of:

Personal liability under your primary home and umbrella policies generally extends worldwide. Therefore, if you accidentally injure someone in Paris or damage property in Tokyo, your umbrella should respond. But always read the fine print, because most policies exclude claims arising from foreign property you own, business activities that you conduct abroad, or vehicles you operate in other countries. Even when coverage applies, enforcing a US policy judgment abroad or satisfying a foreign judgment under US coverage can be complicated.

Personal property coverage under your homeowners policy typically extends to the belongings you travel with, though it usually has sub-limits. Claims are likely to be restricted to around 10 percent of your total contents coverage. That may be adequate for a suitcase of clothes, but it may not stretch to the jewelry, watches, or electronics you might also be carrying. If you have specifically scheduled certain items on your policy, they are usually covered wherever they are in the world. As with most coverage, it's important to verify this before traveling.

Health insurance is where assumptions are most dangerous. Most domestic health plans provide limited or no coverage outside the US. Perhaps yours offers emergency coverage abroad, but it probably requires you to pay out of pocket and seek reimbursement for any treatment you receive.

That might work for a clinic visit, but it's definitely not workable for a serious hospitalization that generates six-figure bills. You should also not rely solely on Medicare, as it provides no coverage outside the US except in narrow circumstances. And almost no domestic health insurance covers *medical evacuation*, should you require emergency transportation to find suitable care outside of the U.S.

Auto insurance also has hard territorial limits. If you are with a standard insurance carrier, your US policy will generally extend throughout the US, Canada, the US Virgin Islands, and certain other US territories, although it's crucial to verify the specifics before traveling. Elsewhere in the world, including Mexico, where US insurance isn't legally recognized, your domestic auto policy provides no coverage at all. Another important point is that when renting vehicles abroad, your personal auto policy most likely excludes international rentals, and credit card coverage varies dramatically by card and country. This is another area where private client carriers shine. Most will give you 30–90 days of liability and property damage coverage for rented vehicles anywhere in the world, excluding only countries with US travel restrictions.

Homeowners coverage does not extend to property in other countries. Your US policy is designed to protect your US home, not homes elsewhere. This is why foreign properties require separate coverage — a topic we'll address in detail shortly.

Workers' compensation for household employees generally only covers work performed in the US, but you should verify this with your carrier. If your nanny travels with you and your family internationally, for example, any injuries they sustain abroad may not be covered under your domestic workers' comp policy.

Finally, watercraft large enough to travel internationally need marine insurance with appropriate *navigational limits*. Sailing beyond those limits without notifying your insurer can void your coverage entirely, so check carefully before embarking. We cover watercraft in detail in Chapter 4.

The pattern for operating on foreign soil is clear: assume nothing in your insurance policies automatically crosses borders. Verify everything before you go.

Temporary Exposure: Risk While Traveling

We have established that international travel creates exposure that domestic coverage isn't designed to address. For most travelers, these risks are manageable with thoughtful preparation. Now let's consider some of the unique exposures that traveling presents and what to do about them:

Medical Risk and Evacuation

The most significant risk you're likely to encounter while traveling is medical. This is not because illness or injury is likely, but because the consequences of needing medical attention abroad can be severe and the costs of obtaining it are extraordinary.

The first point to note is that access to quality healthcare varies dramatically by destination. Major cities in Western Europe, Japan, or Australia generally have excellent facilities. However, if your destination is a rural area in a developing country, it may have clinics that can stabilize you in an emergency but not provide definitive care.

Medical evacuation costs can be astounding, ranging from $50,000 to $250,000 or more, depending on where you are and where you need to go. Air ambulances, medical escorts, specialized equipment, international logistics — none of this is cheap, and almost none of it is covered by domestic health insurance. The Prestons learned this all too well.

The $187,000 Flight

During what was supposed to be a celebratory retirement trip, Richard Preston, 64, suffered a heart attack while hiking in a remote area of Ecuador. The local clinic told him it could stabilize him but couldn't provide the cardiac care he needed, so he had to return to the US. Unfortunately, air evacuation to a hospital in Miami would cost $187,000. Richard's domestic health insurance covered the Miami hospitalization but denied responsibility for the evacuation claim in its entirety. Ultimately, Richard had to pay out of pocket for the flight that saved his life.

Purchasing comprehensive travel insurance addresses the gap in medical evacuation coverage. If you are a frequent international traveler, an annual policy often makes more sense than per-trip coverage — you're never caught unprotected on a spontaneous journey. Companies like Chubb and Allianz offer annual travel policies that can cover your medical needs while traveling.

Security, Detention, and Legal Exposure

Beyond medical risks, international travel exposes travelers to risks most domestic travelers never consider. Setting foot in a new country inevitably brings safety issues and very distinct legal systems. Here are some to consider:

Security risks vary by destination, but they exist everywhere. Whether we're talking about petty crime, violent crime, civil unrest, or terrorism, the probabilities may differ from place to place, but the consequences don't respect your assumptions about which countries might be safe to visit. Situational awareness matters as much abroad as it does at home, so it's important not to drop your guard. Remember, too, that affluent travelers can be targets precisely because of their visible wealth.

Legal exposure abroad also operates under different rules than those you are used to. One area where insurance often comes into play is when Americans are involved in accidents abroad. In the US, accidents are generally civil matters — you might be sued, but you probably won't be arrested. In many other countries, causing an accident resulting in serious bodily injury or death can result in criminal charges, detention, and legal processes that bear little resemblance to the American justice system. Your passport may even be confiscated while investigations proceed.

American embassies and consulates can help you if you fall afoul of local law while abroad, but their powers are limited. They can provide lists of local attorneys, contact members of your family, and monitor the way you are treated by law enforcement agencies — but they cannot get you out of jail, override local law, or provide legal representation. "I'm an American citizen" is not the magic phrase that makes foreign problems disappear, the way you see in old movies.

Kidnap and Ransom (K&R) risk affects more people than you might think. The risk is not limited to executives and their families operating in high-risk regions. If you are an affluent traveler who visibly displays your wealth and maintains predictable behavior while abroad, you might inadvertently increase your exposure more than you intend. If you think that this exposure applies to you, private client insurance carriers usually have coverage options to protect you better while abroad.

Permanent Exposure: Foreign Property and Partial Residency

Owning property abroad is fundamentally different from simply visiting a country. If this applies to you, you're not a mere tourist who needs travel insurance — you're a property owner with ongoing obligations, local legal exposure, and coverage needs that domestic policies don't address.

Why US Policies Don't Apply

Standard policies, and even private client policies to an extent, have territorial limits that typically end at the border when it comes to property that you own outside the US and its territories.

The Uninsured Villa

The Delgados were US citizens who purchased a beautiful property on the coast of Spain. It was to be their vacation home for several months per year and eventually a place they would retire to. Working with a local property attorney on the purchase, they navigated the Spanish legal requirements and gleefully took possession of their dream property.

However, insurance wasn't on their checklist. In their excitement over the purchase, they assumed that they'd figure it out later, but with busy lives, they never circled back to it. Since they weren't carrying a mortgage on the home, no one was requiring proof of coverage to secure the deal.

Eighteen months after the purchase, the wiring to their water heater grounded out, causing a fire that damaged a significant portion of the Spanish villa. Knowing it was a long shot, the Delgados filed a claim with their US insurance carrier, and the carrier confirmed what they had feared. Their policy didn't cover property outside the US.

The repairs cost approximately €180,000, which they had no choice but to cover entirely out of pocket. Had they purchased appropriate Spanish property coverage, the premium would have been just a few thousand euros annually and would have covered the loss.

Obtaining the right coverage for your foreign property means working with local insurers or international carriers with a presence in that market. It's important to check what's available, as some private client carriers offer international property programs. These policies operate across multiple countries with familiar coverage terms and claims handling in English, which can be a huge benefit if your command of the destination language is not fluent. While these programs don't eliminate the need to comply with local rules and legal requirements, they do reduce the complexity of managing your coverage across borders.

Liability Tied to Foreign Property

Picture a scenario where you have invited people over to your overseas property. If one of your guests is injured there, the local law governs any ensuing claim. This means that liability standards and damage calculations may diverge considerably from what you are used to because each jurisdiction is different. Your US umbrella may or may not apply to claims arising from property you own abroad. As we saw in the Delgado story above, many policies, in fact, exclude exactly this situation.

Even if you discover that your umbrella policy does extend to foreign property claims, you may need local liability coverage as well. Some countries require it. In other cases, having it is simply prudent because local coverage is almost always easier to apply to local legal processes.

Residency Creep

Now let's turn to a risk many property owners don't see coming: what happens when you spend so much time at your foreign property that you become a tax resident of that country for all intents and purposes?

Most countries have rules about how long you can stay before you're considered a resident. The thresholds vary — 183 days is common, but not universal — and the consequences of triggering residency can be significant. To start with, you may find you owe taxes in that country. Secondly, you might even become subject to obligations under the local healthcare system. Many countries, such as Germany, Switzerland, Japan, France, and Canada, typically make healthcare contributions mandatory for expats.

The best advice is to track your days carefully if you spend substantial time abroad. What feels like casual use of a vacation property can unintentionally accumulate into residency status. Once you've triggered residency, unwinding the consequences is often difficult and time-consuming.

Your US Properties While You're Away

When international life takes you abroad for extended periods, your US properties don't simply pause. They still require monitoring, maintenance, and compliance with the policies you have set up to cover them.

Vacancy clauses are the most immediate concern. Most standard homeowners policies limit or modify coverage when a property is unoccupied for an extended period — typically 30–60 consecutive days. Go away for more than two months, and you will definitely be in this territory. Going away for this long can reduce or eliminate coverage for certain perils unless specific conditions are met. So, if you're spending three months at your Italian villa, your Connecticut home may cross the vacancy threshold. A quick call to your advisor before an extended trip can prevent an unpleasant surprise later when you might need to make a claim.

Property monitoring becomes essential when you're not there to notice problems yourself. The home safety and monitoring systems that we discussed in Chapter 3 really shine when you're away. For example, smart water leak sensors with automatic shut-off, temperature monitors, and security systems can now typically be monitored and controlled from anywhere in the world. So important are they that these are no longer viewed as just risk reduction — they may be coverage requirements.

Maintenance doesn't stop because you're abroad, either. Landscaping, snow removal, HVAC servicing, and grounds upkeep all continue to matter because deferred maintenance that leads to loss can create coverage disputes. Make sure that you have the proper service agreements in place. If you don't, you'll need to hire a property manager to look after these while you are away.

Building a Coherent International Risk Program

The risk with international exposure is ending up with a patchwork of policies. Unless you are careful, you could end up with coverage from different carriers in different countries with different terms that may not work together when you need them. Below are the steps to work through to shore up your protection at home and abroad.

Start with Your Domestic Program

Before adding international coverage, understand what you already have. The first step is to review your existing policies, such as your umbrella, homeowners, auto, and marine insurance, and identify their territorial limits. What coverage do they provide that would travel with you? What's excluded? Where do the gaps begin?

Add Local Coverage Where Appropriate

For permanent or semi-permanent international exposure, you need coverage in each jurisdiction where you have any significant presence. Here are the key foreign assets you'll need to protect:

Foreign property requires you to possess local property and liability coverage. Your US carrier may offer international programs, or you may need to work with local insurers. Either way, the coverage must comply with local requirements and coordinate with your US program.

Vehicles abroad need local auto coverage if you own or regularly operate vehicles in another country. Don't even consider driving without verified local coverage in any country where your US policy doesn't apply.

If your international exposure is significant, ask your primary risk advisor about their international capabilities. If they can't address your needs directly, they should be coordinating with domestic and overseas specialists who can.

Documentation and Access

We've previously covered the necessity of clear and comprehensive record-keeping for all your insurance coverage. Here are the key actions to take to make your coverage as international as it can be:

- Maintain a master document, listing all your domestic and international coverage, including policy numbers, coverage limits, territorial scope, and claims contacts. Store it somewhere accessible to you and to key family members or advisors from anywhere in the world.

- Know who can act on your behalf if you're incapacitated abroad. Can your spouse access insurance information and initiate claims? International emergencies don't wait for business hours, so the person should be ready to act if needed.

- Maintain sufficient liquidity that can be accessed where needed, in local currencies if necessary. Emergencies in foreign countries require resources you can access from foreign countries, meaning credit cards that work globally, the ability to wire funds internationally, and cash reserves for situations where cards aren't accepted.

The Point of Global Engagement

We all love time abroad, but as much as international life expands your opportunity set, it also expands your exposure. That villa overlooking the Mediterranean, the yacht exploring foreign waters, or the experiences available only through global engagement — these are among the privileges wealth enables.

Your life doesn't stop at the border. Neither should your protection.

The Four Pillars Applied to International Risk

Risk Reduction

- Understand what coverage follows you internationally before you travel.
- Research destinations — healthcare availability, security conditions, and the legal environment.
- Document everything — passport, insurance cards, policy numbers, and emergency contacts.
- Track days carefully to avoid unintentionally triggering residency.
- Maintain foreign properties to local standards with local property managers.
- Arrange monitoring and maintenance for empty US properties during any extended absences.

Risk Transfer

- Obtain local property and liability coverage for foreign real estate.

- Carry comprehensive travel insurance with adequate medical and evacuation coverage.
- Verify your umbrella's international reach; add local liability coverage where appropriate.
- Obtain local auto coverage before driving in countries where US insurance isn't recognized.
- Get written confirmation of how US and foreign policies coordinate.

Risk Avoidance

- Don't drive abroad without verified local coverage.
- Don't acquire foreign property without professional guidance.
- Don't exceed residency thresholds without understanding the consequences.
- Don't assume consular services will solve legal problems abroad.

Risk Retention

- Accept that perfect coordination across borders isn't always possible
- Maintain internationally accessible liquidity for emergencies abroad
- Acknowledge that some international risks may be uninsurable
- Accept that claims abroad will generally be slower and more complicated than domestic claims

In Chapter 11, we step back from specific exposures to see the whole picture. Your insurance policies aren't separate purchases — they're components of a single system that should be managed with the same sophistication you bring to all your investments.

11

Your Private
Insurance Portfolio

Your investment portfolio gets quarterly reviews, professional management, and careful coordination. Your insurance portfolio? Probably less so.

Imagine if you treated your investments the way some people treat their insurance. You'd buy stocks from one broker without telling them about the bonds you bought from another. You'd hold real estate investments that nobody was tracking alongside your securities. You'd have no idea whether your overall allocation made sense, whether gaps existed, or whether you were over-concentrated in some areas. You'd review the whole picture once every few years — maybe — and otherwise just let it run on autopilot.

No sophisticated investor would accept that approach for their financial portfolio. Yet that's exactly how most affluent families manage their risk portfolio. Staggeringly, these savvy and dynamic people often neglect to maintain the insurance policies, risk-management strategies, and protection mechanisms that stand between them and financial catastrophe.

So far in this book, we've examined individual components of risk management, including property coverage and vehicle protection, collections insurance, liability umbrellas, family and legacy planning, and international exposures. Each chapter has addressed a specific category of risk to build up a picture of what defenses you need. But risks don't exist in isolation, so neither should your approach to managing them.

This chapter is about integration. The goal is to view insurance and risk management as a unified portfolio that should be designed, monitored, and organized with the same sophistication you bring to your investments.

Gaps, Misalignments, and Overlaps

Three problems plague insurance portfolios that aren't managed holistically: gaps, misalignments, and overlaps that can develop between policies.

Gaps are the exposures that fall between policies — risks you thought were covered but aren't. They are the umbrella that doesn't attach properly to an underlying auto policy, the expensive watch you bought that exceeds your homeowners sub-limit for jewelry, or the liability exposure from a rental property that your personal umbrella excludes. Often, gaps like these aren't discovered until claims are filed, which is the worst possible time to learn your protection has holes.

Misalignments occur when policies that should work together don't quite fit. Say, for example, that your estate plan assumes your life insurance will provide liquidity when fees and costs become due, but the policy ownership structure means that any proceeds will be taxed as a part of your estate. In this scenario, taxation would erode the liquidity your heirs need most, exactly when they need it. Aditionally, consider the situation in which your international property isn't covered under your domestic umbrella's worldwide coverage. Even a small mishap on that property would leave you paying the bills out of your own pocket. These misalignments create uncertainty about how coverage will respond when you need it most, and they often go undetected.

Overlaps happen when exposures are covered by multiple policies. This isn't necessarily a problem, but you can't be indemnified twice, and it can often lead to an unnecessary expense.

Double Indemnity

On reviewing their outgoing expenses, the Huntsmans discovered they'd been paying for the same jewelry coverage twice. Years earlier, they'd quite reasonably scheduled their valuable pieces on their homeowners policy. Later, after acquiring additional jewelry, a different advisor placed them on a standalone jewelry floater that covered everything, including the pieces they'd already scheduled under the homeowners policy. For four years, they paid premiums on both. In total, the duplication cost them roughly $3,200 in unnecessary premiums — not catastrophic, but wasteful. A single portfolio review, looking at all their coverage together, would have caught it immediately.

Adopting a portfolio approach to insurance helps you identify and address all three concerns. Build in regular portfolio reviews, and you stand a far stronger chance of catching problems before they become claims.

The Annual Portfolio Review

Investment portfolios rightly get reviewed regularly. You want to be certain that your money is working as hard as it can for you. It follows, therefore, that risk portfolios should also be reviewed at least annually.

The annual review isn't just for checking that your premiums have been paid and your policies haven't lapsed. Instead, it should be a comprehensive assessment. This is the time to ask: Has anything changed? Do exposures match existing coverage? Are policy limits still appropriate? Have gaps or misalignments developed since the last review?

If the answers to those questions identify that changes have taken place, you'll need to examine what is different now and upgrade your policies accordingly:

Changes in your life should trigger conversations about coverage. Things you buy or sell need to be accounted for, and the limits in your policies need to be adjusted. These might include renovating or selling a property or vehicle, or buying a new one. Equally, if you are a collector, you might acquire new, valuable items or divest of some of the long-standing pieces frequently. Then there are happy events when your family adds new members or household staff, and sad ones when somebody leaves. You lead a busy life, and that means you'll enter new business ventures or accept board positions, and it might also extend your responsibilities overseas, perhaps in terms of extended travel or owning international property. Any material change in your life may affect your risk profile, so it's essential to discuss it with your insurance provider.

Changes in your net worth should trigger a review of your limits. As your wealth grows, your liability exposure necessarily increases. Your newfound visibility makes you a more attractive target, and the consequences of inadequate protection become more severe. Umbrella limits that made sense even five years ago may be inadequate today.

Economic changes should also be considered, as markets can be volatile and respond rapidly to geopolitical events. If you are engaged in building projects or renovations and construction costs rise midway, that will affect the adequacy of your existing property coverage. When it comes to collections, what was highly sought after 10 years ago might be out of favor today, so your coverage should reflect that. Coverage that was appropriate when the asset was purchased may drift out of alignment with current values. If that happens, you will either find yourself seriously exposed with inadequate coverage or paying far too much for a policy you don't need.

Gap Closed

The Thorntons had worked with the same insurance advisor for eight years. Every fall, they conducted an annual review — a practice the advisor insisted on, and one the Thorntons initially found excessive but came to value.

During their ninth review, the advisor noticed something odd. That spring, the Thorntons had purchased a lake house — a property they'd talked about casually when they were house shopping, but hadn't formally discussed with their advisor.

They'd given the address to someone at some point, they thought. Sadly, they hadn't. The property had no coverage at all. For six months, a $1.2 million home had been completely uninsured. It had no property coverage, no liability coverage, nothing. A fire, an injured guest, or any significant event would have been a huge exposure for them.

Now that it was caught during their annual review, their advisor was able to write a new policy for the home, and the gap was quickly closed. But had that review not happened when it did, and had the Thorntons been the type of family to let policies auto-renew without examination, the home might have stayed uninsured indefinitely.

Regular reviews, done right, provide your best chance of catching what casual attention misses.

Get the Most from Your Annual Review

The Annual Review Preparation Checklist in the Appendix helps you arrive to your annual review prepared. It covers what documents to gather, what changes to report, and what questions to ask. A review is only as productive as the preparation that goes into it. Download the fillable PDF version at www.fortifiedbook.com/resources so you can use it year after year.

Documentation That Works

Maintain a master summary. A single document that lists all your policies, coverage types, limits, deductibles, premiums, renewal dates, and contact information. When your insurance policies change, you should update your master list, which makes an annual review essential. Make this document accessible to your spouse, your advisor, and anyone who might need to act on your behalf.

Keep supporting documentation organized. At a minimum, it should be clear where to find the home inventory that supports your property coverage, the appraisals that evidence your scheduled valuables, and any photographs that document your collections. Good documentation transforms disputed claims into straightforward ones.

Consider what would happen if you were suddenly incapacitated. Could your spouse manage the insurance portfolio? Could your executor? If the answers to these questions are uncertain, your documentation needs work.

Your Risk Advisor's Place at the Table

Managing a portfolio of this scale requires a specialist — someone who can see the whole picture, identify gaps, and coordinate across all your coverage. They should form an integral part of your advisory team alongside your attorney, investment manager, business advisor, and property manager.

There are very good reasons for looking holistically across your portfolio. Your estate plan affects how policies should be titled and who should own them. Your investment strategy affects the liability exposure that needs to be covered. Your tax planning affects how your life insurance should be structured. Your business activities create exposures that need to be contemplated in your personal program. When your advisors work in silos, gaps form between their specialties. When they collaborate, those gaps get caught.

For these cogs in the machine to work together, someone will need to convene the conversation — whether that's you, your family office, or an advisor you've empowered to coordinate matters on your behalf. The risk advisor who has a seat at the table, who knows what your estate attorney is planning and what your wealth advisor is recommending, can design protection that truly fits your complete situation. One who only sees their own slice will miss the places where insurance intersects with everything else.

In Chapter 12, we turn to the question of who helps you build and maintain this system. The complexity we've discussed throughout this book exceeds what anyone can realistically manage on their own. Finding the right specialist — and building a relationship that serves you for years — matters enormously.

12

The Specialist

However good they are at technical support, you wouldn't ask the Geek Squad to put an astronaut into orbit.

Not that I'm pretending that private client risk management is rocket science. If it were, I'd have a much cooler view out of my office window and a funkier haircut. No, this is more like being the ground crew for someone else's moonshot: we check the seals, calibrate the thrusters (read: check for coverage gaps and calibrate complete risk management plans), and make sure nothing blows up mid-flight. This means your average insurance agent might handle the basics just fine. But when your net worth has escape velocity of its own, you want the specialists who live for the complicated trajectories — not the ones who panic when the dashboard lights up.

I have tremendous respect for this industry and its professionals. After all, I've made lifelong friends and trusted collaborators among risk managers across the US and Canada. That said, agents come in all stripes, and by 2026, estimates suggest there are somewhere between 900,000 and 1 million of us. In a field where three weeks of studying and achieving 70 percent on a licensing exam can get you a job, it follows that not all risk advisors are equal.

Why Work with a Private Client Insurance Specialist

The same basic concepts apply whether you're insuring a $200,000 starter home or a $20 million estate. In essence, you transfer risk to an insurance carrier in exchange for the premium you pay. But the similarities end there.

High-net-worth insurance is an entirely different business. In this world, exposures are amplified and more diverse: multi-property portfolios, supercars, yachts, and aircraft; significant liability targets; household staff; and international activities, making for a far more complex profile. It stands to reason that the products that address these exposures must also differ. They need to offer protection such as guaranteed replacement cost and cash-out coverage for your $15 million home; umbrella policies in the tens of millions; specialized forms for jewelry, art, and wine collections; and policies that provide agreed-value settlements for exotic and classic cars, aircraft, and yachts. These are not the generic policies that get written in 15 minutes. Products and coverage are unique, so the carriers that provide them are also very different. These companies possess *underwriting* expertise, claims handling, and risk management services designed specifically for complex clients — and they limit access to a relatively small group of specialized risk advisors.

An advisor whose practice centers on Main Street accounts may not have access to these carriers, may not recognize coverage gaps because they rarely write the forms that fit this audience, and may not spot exposures that are routine for affluent families but rare in their typical book. This isn't a criticism — they serve their market well. Their market just isn't yours.

But the specialist provides protection — coverage designed for your own situation, with gaps identified and addressed, and terms that are understood and appropriate. That difference matters greatly when something goes wrong.

What to Look for in a Specialist

How can you know if an advisor you are working with is right for you? There are some important criteria an advisor should fulfill to win your business:

Focus and Experience

The most important indicator is focus. Find out what portion of the advisor's practice involves clients like you. An advisor whose high-net-worth clients represent only 10 percent of their clientele may be a generalist dabbling in the space. Whereas an advisor whose practice is entirely focused on affluent families has specialized experience you can't get anywhere else.

Ask potential advisors about their typical client and the range of their clients' net worth. They should be able to provide examples of the types of assets involved and the complexity of their clients' situations. The answers to these questions will reveal whether their experience matches your needs.

You also need to know about their experience with situations like yours. They should be comfortable handling homes, collections, or liability exposures like your own. If you have unusual circumstances, such as an interest in property over-seas, a significant public profile, or complex family structures, ask them about their specific experience with those.

An important distinction is that years in the business matter less than the years spent focused on this market. Someone with five years of experience exclusively serving affluent clients likely has more relevant experience than someone with 20 years of experience working in general insurance who occasionally handles the portfolio of a wealthy family.

Carrier Access

Because of its unique characteristics, the high-net-worth insurance market is served by specific carriers — such as PURE, Chubb, Cincinnati Insurance, Berkley One, Selective, Private Client Select, and a few others — that offer dedicated programs for affluent families. These carriers offer coverage forms, claims handling, and risk management services that standard carriers can't and don't match.

The advisor you select should have demonstrable access to these markets. Ask them which carriers they work with. If they're primarily placing coverage with standard carriers, they may not have the appointments or expertise to access the private client market, which could leave you without the protection you need.

Access to multiple carriers matters too. Different carriers have different strengths — some excel in certain geographies, some have better coverage for specific exposures, while others have superior claims handling. An advisor with access to and knowledge of multiple private client carriers can match your situation to the carrier best suited for it, rather than fitting you into whatever coverage they can place.

Approach and Process

When selecting your new advisor, pay attention to how they approach the relationship. A specialist will ask detailed questions about your assets, activities, family, business interests, and concerns before making any recommendations. They'll want to review your existing coverage and take time to design a program rather than just quote policies. If someone is ready to give you prices before they've truly learned about your situation, they're selling products, not designing protection.

Look for an advisor who thinks beyond policies. By now, you should understand that smart risk management isn't just about buying insurance — it's about evaluating each exposure you face in turn and deciding the best way to handle them. Your advisor may not use the same framework or terminology you've learned in this book, but they should be thinking about providing coverage in the same way. If every conversation leads to "This is the insurance product you should buy," without ever discussing how to reduce or transfer a risk, whether to avoid it entirely, or when it makes sense to retain it yourself, you're not getting the full picture.

Be sure to ask an advisor about their ongoing service model. You need to understand how they would handle annual reviews and stay abreast of changes in your life. This extends to how they would manage claims, when you would be likely to hear from them, and how often. The relationship extends far beyond the initial placement, so make sure the ongoing service also matches your expectations.

Team and Resources

Even excellent individual advisors have limitations. For example, a sole practitioner may lack backup when they're unavailable. And a small operation whose team isn't also focused on private client risk management may not have the resources to assist when faced with unusual situations.

Ask about the team. If you agree to work with the agency, who else would be involved in your account? And if your primary contact is unavailable — what happens then? Will you have a team working for you or one advisor?

Resources matter too. Does the firm have access to specialists for the unusual types of coverage that might matter to you, such as marine, aviation, fine art, or international exposures? Would they have claims advocacy capabilities if you needed help with a difficult claim? Do they provide risk management services or consultation beyond just placing coverage? Ideally, you want an advisor who is backed by an organization, not just an individual who might retire, relocate, or become unavailable when you need them.

Coordination with Other Advisors

A great advisor understands they're not working in isolation on your portfolio. Your risk management program inevitably touches your estate plan, investment strategy, business interests, and household staff. Therefore, the best specialists want to know who else advises you, from your wealth manager, your estate attorney, and your family office to your executive assistant — and they're comfortable coordinating with them all. They'll want to understand how your insurance coverage will interact with your trust structures, how any claims might affect liquidity, and how employment practices in your household might create exposure. If an advisor treats insurance as a silo, they're missing the connections that matter.

Questions to Ask Potential Advisors

When interviewing potential advisors, certain questions are very helpful in revealing their capability and fit:

About their practice:

Q. What percentage of your clients would you describe as high-net-worth?

Q. What's the typical net worth and asset profile of your clients?

Q. How long have you focused on this market?

Q. How many clients do you personally handle, and do you have the capacity to give proper attention to new relationships?

About their expertise:

Q. What carriers do you work with in the private client space?

Q. How do you stay current on coverage developments and market changes?

Q. What designations or continuing education do you maintain?

Q. Can you describe a complex situation you've handled recently that's like mine?

About their process:

Q. How would you approach gaining an understanding of my situation?

Q. What does your discovery process look like?

Q. How do you identify gaps in your clients' existing coverage?

Q. How do you determine appropriate policy limits and coverage structures?

About ongoing service:

Q. How often do you conduct policy reviews?

Q. How might you learn about changes in my situation that would affect coverage?

Q. Who's my backup when you're unavailable?

About references:

Q. Can you provide references from clients with situations like mine?

Q. Can you share examples of problems you've identified and solved for clients?

The quality of their answers matter, but so too does the quality of the questions they ask you. An advisor who asks thoughtful, detailed questions about your situation is likely to understand what information they need to serve you well.

Building a Productive Relationship

Finding the right advisor is only the beginning. To succeed, the relationship requires ongoing attention from both sides.

Your Responsibilities

As we discussed in Chapter 11, your advisor can only protect what they know about. Here's a brief recap:

New acquisitions should be reported to your advisor promptly. A new property, a new vehicle, a significant addition to your collection, or a newly acquired valuable piece of jewelry will all need coverage, and coverage can't begin until your advisor knows about them. Don't assume anything is automatically protected.

Changes in how you use assets matter. The vacation home you've started renting out, the vehicle now being driven by a household employee while performing their duties, the property undergoing renovation. Use affects coverage, and changes in use need to be communicated.

Life changes should also trigger conversations with your advisor. If you have welcomed a new family member or accepted a new board position, you may want to let your advisor know. Similarly, a new business venture or increased international travel to new destinations may all have insurance implications that your advisor should evaluate.

Participate in reviews. When your advisor schedules an annual review, make time for it. Come prepared to discuss changes, concerns, and questions. The review only works if you engage with it and provide the information your advisor needs. Use the Annual Review Preparation Checklist in the Appendix to prepare. It ensures you bring what your advisor needs, and you can leave with the answers to the questions that matter most. A fillable PDF version is available at www.fortifiedbook.com/resources.

What to Expect from Your Advisor

In return, you should expect a genuine partnership. This includes:

Proactive communication. Your advisor should initiate contact rather than merely react to your prompts. This includes being there not just when policies renew, but when they see something relevant to your situation, when markets change in ways that might affect you, or when they have new ideas for improving your program.

Responsive service. When you reach out, your questions should be answered promptly and your policy changes processed efficiently. They should provide all the certificates and documentation you need without you having to repeatedly request them.

Advocacy when you need it. If you must make a claim, your advisor should be involved throughout: helping you navigate the process, pushing back if the carrier isn't treating you fairly, and ensuring you receive what you're entitled to.

Red Flags to Watch out for

Certain behaviors suggest an advisor may not be right for your situation:

Difficulty explaining coverage. You should understand what you're buying. An advisor who can't explain coverage clearly either doesn't understand it themselves or isn't prioritizing your comprehension of the situation or how to handle it.

Disappearing after the sale. If your advisor is highly attentive during the sales process but hard to reach afterward, their priority is transactions, not relationships.

Lack of curiosity about your situation. Great advisors are genuinely interested in understanding your life, your concerns, and your goals. If your advisor seems to be going through the motions, you're not getting their best work.

When to Make a Change

Loyalty to a long-time advisor is admirable, but not if it comes at the cost of comprehensive protection.

Consider a change if:

Your situation has outgrown your advisor's expertise or their carrier's capabilities. When an agent struggles to answer your questions — or when the best solution they can offer is a standard policy that doesn't fit — the growth in your wealth and lifestyle has outpaced the relationship.

Service has deteriorated. Slow responses, missed renewals, and coverage errors are signs that an advisor is either overextended or no longer prioritizing your relationship.

You've lost confidence. Trust is vital in this relationship. If you're not confident that your advisor is looking out for your interests, acting competently, or keeping up to date on your situation, the relationship isn't working.

Making a change isn't complicated. You can move coverage to a new advisor at any time without incurring a penalty. Your new advisor will be able to handle the practicalities of the transition. The hardest part is often the emotional difficulty of ending a long relationship — but your protection is too important for sentiment to override substance when it comes to securing the right insurance for you and your family.

The Expert in Your Corner

Without question, finding the right specialist requires effort. You'll need to ask a lot of questions, evaluate the answers you receive, and check references before you can even get to building a relationship.

In our final chapter, we bring everything together. The concepts, the types of coverage, the framework, and the specialists — all of it integrates into a comprehensive approach to risk management that offers more than mere protection. It provides confidence, clarity, and control. Let's bring it home.

13

Bringing It Home

We began this book with a simple observation: that your life has likely grown more complex than the protection previously designed for it.

Many families never notice when they cross that line. They renew policies suited to simpler times, assuming that "comprehensive coverage" still means what it used to. But as you've learned throughout these chapters, it often doesn't.

You now understand that liability exposure scales with wealth and that umbrella limits that were adequate five years ago may be dangerously insufficient today. We've also discovered significant differences between mass-market insurance policies and those for high-net-worth individuals. It seems obvious when put like this: coverage must align with how you use your assets, not just what you own on paper. Yet that simple truth is often misunderstood.

Along the way, we've explored the Four Pillars of Risk Management. Risk Reduction, Risk Transfer, Risk Avoidance, and Risk Retention — and we've seen how they can be applied across every category of exposure in your life. That means every category, including your properties, vehicles, collections, household operations, liability profile, reputation, family legacy, and your international activities. Now it's time to bring it all together.

The Fortified Life

A fortified life isn't about fear. It isn't about building walls so high you can't enjoy what's on the other side. Nor is it about obsessing over everything that could go wrong. It's about preparation that paves the way for freedom.

When your vacation home is properly insured, meaning you have adequate liability that is coordinated with your umbrella, you can enjoy it. There's no doubt lurking in the back of your mind about whether you're really protected if something happens. When your art collection is scheduled, documented, and covered for the perils that matter, you can display the pieces you own and love without anxiety. And when your vehicles carry appropriate policy limits, and your umbrella extends to all of them, you can drive with confidence.

This is what wealth is supposed to provide: the freedom to live fully, unburdened by the constant low-level worry that accompanies unmanaged risk. The families who achieve this aren't lucky — they're prepared. They've done the work to understand their exposures, close coverage gaps, and build protection that matches their unique lives.

These individuals approach risk systematically, address it thoroughly, and then stop thinking about it. That's the fortified life. Protection that fades into the background because it's solid enough to trust.

The Four Pillars provide a structure for thinking about every risk you'll encounter — not just the ones we've discussed in this book, but for every exposure you'll face for the rest of your life.

The pillars interlock, and with these risk management fundamentals in place, you reduce what you can, you transfer what would otherwise be catastrophic, you avoid what isn't worth the exposure, and you retain what's manageable. Applied together, they create comprehensive protection that's also efficient — you're not over-insuring minor risks or under-insuring major ones.

The Integration Imperative

Fragmentation is the silent killer in risk management. As we saw in Chapter 11, none of your insurance coverage exists in a vacuum. Your property coverage and your auto limits affect your umbrella policy. Your international exposures create gaps that domestic policies weren't designed to address. Your ownership of life insurance affects your estate taxes, and your household employment practices also create liability that needs to be contemplated somewhere in your program.

When you treat each policy as a separate purchase, disconnected from everything else, gaps inevitably form. You might have excellent property coverage, excellent auto coverage, and excellent umbrella coverage — and still have a gap where one policy ends and another begins.

Families that are genuinely protected treat their risk portfolio as an interconnected system. They understand how the pieces fit together and ensure coordination among them. Sound oversight means that underlying policy limits always satisfy umbrella requirements, that all property and vehicles are scheduled where they need to be, that coverage forms are compatible, and that nothing falls through the cracks. And they ensure their risk advisor has a seat at the table alongside their other trusted advisors, rather than operating in isolation.

This integration doesn't happen automatically. It requires someone — you, a family member, or an advisor you trust — to see the whole picture and verify that the pieces genuinely work together. It also requires periodic review because your life changes, and the coverage coordinated last year may already be out of alignment. So much can happen in 12 months.

Integrated protection is what delivers real security. If your coverage is fragmented, it creates the illusion of protection that evaporates when you need it most.

Ongoing Discipline

Risk management isn't a project with an end date. It's a discipline to be maintained, not something you complete before moving on. Your circumstances change constantly, so your risk management approach should too. It must adapt to the properties you acquire or sell. To the vehicles you add and those you replace, as well as the collections that grow in value. There will be changes — some of them dramatic — in net worth, and family situations that evolve through marriage, divorce, birth, and death. Business ventures will be launched or exited, and international activities will expand or contract.

Each change potentially affects your risk profile. Families that maintain genuine protection treat life transitions as automatic triggers for coverage reviews. Something significant changed, so they're reviewing their protection. Not waiting for renewal. Not assuming someone else is handling it.

Annual reviews matter even when nothing dramatic appears to have happened. Prices drift. Markets move. Your situation continues to evolve in ways that aren't obvious until you look carefully. That's why a thorough annual review that walks through your complete risk portfolio, examining each component and verifying coordination, is the best way to catch the gaps that accumulate over time.

Your relationship with a risk advisor and their team is ongoing, not transactional. You need to let them know promptly when things change. In return, they should be proactive in reviewing your situation and available by phone whenever questions arise. This relationship, maintained over the years, is one of your most valuable risk-management assets.

Now You're Equipped

You're now prepared for conversations you couldn't have envisaged before reading this book. You know what questions to ask your insurance advisor and can discuss agreed value versus replacement cost, understand why certain limits matter, and evaluate whether the recommendations they give you will serve your interests.

You understand that insurance and estate planning must coordinate and that life insurance ownership affects whether proceeds are included in your taxable estate, that trust structures affect asset protection, and even that beneficiary designations control where policy proceeds go. The conversations between your insurance advisor and your estate attorney become richer and more productive when you understand both dimensions and can ensure they work together.

You recognize the importance of having the family conversations that many families avoid. The need to prepare heirs for the responsibility that comes with wealth, discuss values around stewardship, and hold the difficult discussions that prevent conflict after you're gone. These conversations don't have to be avoided. The families that handle wealth transitions successfully are the ones that talk about it beforehand.

And perhaps most importantly, you can now honestly assess your own exposures and address the gaps you've been avoiding. Hand on heart, you know that the umbrella limit has been too low for a while. You also know that there are new collectibles that you've never gotten around to scheduling. Weather patterns have changed recently, yet there is flood insurance you've been meaning to purchase for some time, and haven't. You now realize it will all be so much easier to manage and delegate if you take the time to create documentation detailing your policies. You now have the knowledge to act — and no excuse not to.

What Constitutes a Protected Family

Protected families aren't families that never experience losses. Everyone does, eventually. Fire, theft, accidents, lawsuits, market downturns, or health crises — life happens to everyone, regardless of wealth. What sets protected families apart is that the losses they sustain don't become catastrophes.

These families have coverage that is ready to respond when claims are filed — not policies full of gaps and exclusions that emerge only at the worst possible moment. Their documentation proves what they owned and what it was worth — not a mishmash of vague memories and missing receipts. They have advisors who truly advocate for them — not adjusters trying to minimize payouts. For them, structures are in place that protect assets across generations — their wealth is not exposed to every claim that comes along. The difference between devastation and inconvenience often comes down to decisions made years before the loss occurred.

Of course, a house fire is traumatic, but with proper coverage, a family can rebuild their property without financial strain. Every lawsuit is stressful, but the family with adequate liability limits and a vigorous defense won't lose their life's work. And death in the family is devastating, but the family with coordinated estate planning and adequate life insurance isn't left scrambling to pay taxes or settle debts while they grieve.

This is what protection looks like in practice. It's not the absence of adversity, but the ability to weather it.

Confidence, Clarity, Control

Proper risk management provides three things that money alone cannot buy:

Confidence: Knowing that you're genuinely protected. That if a catastrophic event occurs, your coverage will respond. That the people you love won't be financially devastated by a loss. That you've done what can be done to secure what you've built. This isn't false confidence based on assumptions — it's real confidence based on understanding.

Clarity: Knowing exactly where you stand and understanding what's been transferred to insurers or legal instruments and what you're retaining. You know what the limits, deductibles, and exclusions in your policies are. No more wondering whether you're protected or vague hope that someone else is handling it. You know — specifically and precisely — what your protection really provides.

Control: Actively managing your risk rather than passively hoping for the best. This way, you can make deliberate choices about what to insure, what to retain, and what to avoid. You can adjust your coverage as your life evolves, rather than letting policies auto-renew, unaware of the changing landscape of your life. You're driving the process, not being driven by it.

These three things — confidence, clarity, and control — transform risk management from a burden into a source of peace. From being a source of worry, it becomes something that frees you from it. A matter settled. A problem solved. Protection that is solid enough to stop thinking about.

What to Do Next

Knowledge without action is just information. Here are five steps to make a strong start:

1. **Find a Private Client Risk Advisor.** Use the criteria laid out in Chapter 12 to identify someone who genuinely focuses on high-net-worth insurance and will serve as your advocate. This relationship is foundational.
2. **Complete the Personal Risk Audit.** The checklist in the Appendix helps you prepare for a conversation with your risk advisor. It gathers valuable information they'll need to evaluate your situation — and gets you thinking about risk management, not just insurance quotes. Complete it before your first meeting, and update it annually. A fillable PDF version is available at www.fortifiedbook.com/resources.
3. **Have one conversation you've been avoiding.** Estate planning with your spouse. Family wealth conversation with your children. Coverage concerns with your advisor. Pick one. Have it this week.
4. **Close one gap you've known about.** The umbrella limit that hasn't kept pace. The unscheduled collectibles. The flood insurance. The

workers' compensation for household staff. Pick the most significant and address it now.

5. **Schedule your annual review.** Make it recurring, not reactive. Put it in your calendar and your risk advisor's. Treat it with the same seriousness you'd give an investment review. Use the Annual Review Preparation Checklist in the Appendix to arrive prepared — a fillable PDF version is available at www.fortifiedbook.com/resources.

You don't have to do everything at once. The goal isn't an overnight transformation — it's systematic improvement. Start with what matters most and build from there.

Welcome to the Fortified Life

You've built something remarkable. The wealth you've accumulated didn't happen by accident. It represents years of effort, countless smart decisions, probably some fortunate timing, and certainly some sacrifice along the way.

That wealth is not just a trophy. It supports your family and enables a lifestyle you've worked hard to achieve. It will benefit generations to come — if it's protected. That protection ought to be as thoughtful as the effort that you put into all those early years. Not slender coverage that was purchased hastily and renewed automatically. Not policies accumulated over time without coordination. And certainly not gaps hidden in fine print that only emerge when disaster strikes.

Reward yourself with real protection. Deliberate protection that is designed for the life you live, with limits that match your actual exposure, and coordinated into a system that works as a coherent whole.

That's what a fortified life provides. Not the absence of risk — that's impossible. But the knowledge that you've addressed what can be addressed, transferred what should be transferred, and prepared your family to weather whatever comes.

You've read this book. You understand the framework. You know the questions to ask and the gaps to look for. You have the knowledge to act.

Now act.

You've earned it.

Appendix

Personal Risk Audit

This audit helps you prepare for a conversation with your risk advisor. It gathers helpful information they'll need to evaluate your situation and design appropriate protection. Just as importantly, it shifts your thinking from shopping for quotes to thinking about risk management — which assets you have, what exposures they create, and what concerns keep you up at night.

A fillable PDF version you can save and share with your advisor is available at www.fortifiedbook.com/resources.

PERSONAL RISK AUDIT

A Comprehensive Self-Assessment for High-Net-Worth Individuals

This audit is designed to help you systematically evaluate your risk exposures and identify gaps in your protection. Complete each section honestly, then bring this document to your advisor meeting.

SECTION 1: PROPERTY EXPOSURES

Primary Residence

☐ Current home value: $___________________

☐ Current Dwelling coverage: $___________________

☐ Extended/Guaranteed replacement cost endorsement in place? ☐ Yes ☐ No ☐ Uncertain

☐ Loss of use coverage: ☐ Capped at $________ ☐ Unlimited ☐ Uncertain

☐ Major renovations in past 5 years? ☐ Yes ☐ No

☐ Any applicable trusts, LLCs or other entities listed on policy? ☐ Yes ☐ No ☐ Uncertain

Notes: ____

Additional Properties (list each)

☐ Property 1: ____________________________ Value: $__________ Type: ☐ Secondary ☐ Rental

☐ Property 2: ____________________________ Value: $__________ Type: ☐ Secondary ☐ Rental

☐ Property 3: ____________________________ Value: $__________ Type: ☐ Secondary ☐ Rental

Notes: ____

Location-Specific Perils

☐ Flood insurance in place where needed? ☐ Yes ☐ No ☐ N/A

☐ Earthquake coverage in place? ☐ Yes ☐ No ☐ N/A

☐ Windstorm/Hurricane coverage adequate? ☐ Yes ☐ No ☐ N/A

☐ Wildfire zone mitigation completed? ☐ Yes ☐ No ☐ N/A

Notes: ____

Property Usage

☐ Any short-term rental activity (Airbnb, VRBO)? ☐ Yes ☐ No → If yes, specific coverage in place? ☐ Yes ☐ No

☐ Home-based business activity? ☐ Yes ☐ No → If yes, business pursuits endorsement? ☐ Yes ☐ No

Notes: ____

Risk Reduction Measures

☐ Water leak detection system installed? ☐ Yes ☐ No

☐ Automatic water shut-off device installed? ☐ Yes ☐ No

☐ Monitored fire and burglar security system? ☐ Yes ☐ No

☐ Backup power/generator? ☐ Yes ☐ No

☐ Fire suppression system? ☐ Yes ☐ No

☐ Last carrier risk assessment date: ___________________

Notes: ____

SECTION 2: VEHICLE EXPOSURES

Auto Liability Coverage

☐ Current liability limits: $____________ per person / $____________ per accident

☐ Limits adequate relative to net worth? ☐ Yes ☐ No ☐ Uncertain

☐ Uninsured/Underinsured motorist coverage: $____________

☐ Uninsured/Underinsured motorist limits match liability limits? ☐ Yes ☐ No

☐ Any applicable trusts, LLCs or other entities listed on policy? ☐ Yes ☐ No ☐ Uncertain

Notes: ____

Vehicle Inventory

☐ Total vehicles (count): ____ Highest vehicle value: $____________

☐ Luxury/Exotic vehicles (count): ____

☐ Collector/Classic vehicles (count): ____

☐ Collector vehicles on agreed value policies? ☐ Yes ☐ No ☐ Uncertain

☐ Agreed values reviewed in past 12 months? ☐ Yes ☐ No

Notes: ____

Other Vehicles & Equipment

☐ Motorcycles: ☐ Yes (count: ____) ☐ No

☐ ATVs/UTVs: ☐ Yes (count: ____) ☐ No

☐ Golf Carts: ☐ Yes (count: ____) ☐ No

☐ Snowmobiles: ☐ Yes (count: ____) ☐ No

☐ All recreational vehicles properly insured? ☐ Yes ☐ No ☐ Uncertain

Notes: ____

Drivers

☐ Teen drivers in household? ☐ Yes ☐ No → If yes, completed driver training? ☐ Yes ☐ No

☐ Household staff who drive your vehicles? ☐ Yes ☐ No → Included on policy? ☐ Yes ☐ No

☐ Regular permissive users outside household? ☐ Yes ☐ No

Notes: ____

SECTION 3: COLLECTIONS & VALUABLES

Jewelry & Watches

☐ Total estimated value: $__________

☐ Scheduled on policy? ☐ Yes, all ☐ Partially ☐ No ☐ Relying on sub-limits

☐ Current sub-limit if not scheduled: $__________

☐ Appraisals current (within 3 years)? ☐ Yes ☐ No

☐ Mysterious disappearance coverage? ☐ Yes ☐ No ☐ Uncertain

☐ Pairs and sets coverage? ☐ Yes ☐ No ☐ Uncertain

Notes: ____

Fine Art

☐ Total estimated value: $__________

☐ Scheduled with agreed values? ☐ Yes ☐ No

☐ Breakage coverage included? ☐ Yes ☐ No

☐ Transit coverage for loans/moves? ☐ Yes ☐ No ☐ N/A

☐ Climate control in display/storage areas? ☐ Yes ☐ No

Notes: ____

Wine Collection

☐ Total estimated value: $__________

☐ Spoilage coverage in place? ☐ Yes ☐ No ☐ Uncertain

☐ Temperature monitoring/alarm? ☐ Yes ☐ No

☐ Backup power for climate control? ☐ Yes ☐ No

Notes: ____

Other Collections (firearms, antiques, memorabilia, etc.)

☐ Collection type: _____________________ Value: $__________ Scheduled? ☐ Yes ☐ No

☐ Collection type: _____________________ Value: $__________ Scheduled? ☐ Yes ☐ No

Notes: ____

Documentation

☐ Comprehensive photo/video inventory exists? ☐ Yes ☐ No

☐ Inventory stored off-site (cloud/safe deposit box)? ☐ Yes ☐ No

☐ Purchase receipts retained? ☐ Yes ☐ Partially ☐ No

☐ Certificates of authenticity secured? ☐ Yes ☐ N/A

☐ Last documentation update: __________________

Notes: ____

SECTION 4: LIABILITY EXPOSURES

Umbrella/Excess Liability

☐ Current umbrella limit: $___________

☐ Approximate net worth: $___________

☐ Umbrella coverage adequate for net worth? ☐ Yes ☐ No

☐ Last umbrella limit review date: _____________________

☐ Underlying auto limits meet umbrella requirements? ☐ Yes ☐ No ☐ Uncertain

☐ Underlying home limits meet umbrella requirements? ☐ Yes ☐ No ☐ Uncertain

☐ Any applicable trusts, LLCs or other entities listed on policy? ☐ Yes ☐ No ☐ Uncertain

Notes: ____

Umbrella Coverage Extensions

☐ Watercraft covered under umbrella? ☐ Yes ☐ No ☐ Uncertain

☐ Recreational vehicles covered? ☐ Yes ☐ No ☐ Uncertain

☐ Personal injury (defamation, etc.) included? ☐ Yes ☐ No ☐ Uncertain

☐ Employment practices liability included? ☐ Yes ☐ No ☐ Uncertain

Notes: ____

Premises Liability Features

☐ Swimming pool? ☐ Yes ☐ No → If yes, fenced with self-closing gate? ☐ Yes ☐ No

☐ Trampoline? ☐ Yes ☐ No → If yes, disclosed to insurer? ☐ Yes ☐ No

☐ Dogs (any breed)? ☐ Yes ☐ No → Breeds: _____________________ Bite history? ☐ Yes ☐ No

☐ Horses? ☐ Yes ☐ No → Separate equine liability? ☐ Yes ☐ No

☐ Playground/sporting equipment? ☐ Yes ☐ No

☐ Pond/lake on property? ☐ Yes ☐ No

Notes: ____

Board Service & Professional Activities

☐ Serve on corporate boards? ☐ Yes ☐ No → D&O coverage verified? ☐ Yes ☐ No

☐ Serve on nonprofit boards? ☐ Yes ☐ No → D&O coverage verified? ☐ Yes ☐ No

☐ HOA board service? ☐ Yes ☐ No

☐ Professional activities creating personal exposure? ☐ Yes ☐ No

Notes: ____

SECTION 5: HOUSEHOLD EMPLOYMENT

Current Household Staff

☐ Full-time employees (count): _____

☐ Part-time employees (count): _____

☐ Live-in employees (count): _____

☐ Positions: ☐ Housekeeper ☐ Nanny ☐ Gardener ☐ Personal Assistant ☐ Chef ☐ Driver ☐ Estate Manager

☐ Other: _____________________

Notes: ____

Compliance & Coverage

☐ All workers properly classified (employee vs. contractor)? ☐ Yes ☐ No ☐ Uncertain

☐ Payroll taxes being withheld and paid? ☐ Yes ☐ No ☐ Using payroll service

☐ Workers' compensation insurance in place? ☐ Yes ☐ No

☐ Employment practices liability coverage? ☐ Yes ☐ No

☐ Written employee handbook exists? ☐ Yes ☐ No

☐ Background checks conducted on all employees? ☐ Yes ☐ No

☐ I-9 forms on file for all employees? ☐ Yes ☐ No

Notes: ____

SECTION 6: LUXURY RECREATIONAL ASSETS

Watercraft

☐ Own watercraft? ☐ Yes ☐ No

☐ Vessel 1: _____________________________ Value: $___________ Hull coverage: $___________

☐ Vessel 2: _____________________________ Value: $___________ Hull coverage: $___________

☐ P&I (liability) limits: $___________

☐ Agreed value coverage? ☐ Yes ☐ No

☐ Navigation limits understood? ☐ Yes ☐ No

☐ Captain/crew requirements met? ☐ Yes ☐ No ☐ N/A

☐ Charter activity? ☐ Yes ☐ No → If yes, commercial coverage? ☐ Yes ☐ No

Notes: ____

Aircraft

☐ Own aircraft? ☐ Yes ☐ No

☐ Aircraft: _____________________________ Value: $___________ Hull coverage: $___________

☐ Liability limits: $___________

☐ Pilot warranty requirements understood and met? ☐ Yes ☐ No

☐ Territorial limits appropriate for planned use? ☐ Yes ☐ No

Notes: ____

Exotic/High-Value Vehicles

☐ Exotic vehicles requiring specialty coverage (list):
____

☐ Covered through specialty market (not standard auto)? ☐ Yes ☐ No

☐ Track day coverage needed? ☐ Yes ☐ No → In place? ☐ Yes ☐ No

☐ Agreed values current? ☐ Yes ☐ No

Notes: ____

Current Protection

☐ Personal cyber insurance policy in place? ☐ Yes ☐ No ☐ Uncertain

☐ If yes, coverage includes: ☐ Wire fraud ☐ Identity theft ☐ Extortion ☐ Privacy breach

☐ Policy limits: $__________

Notes: ____

Security Practices

☐ Password manager in use? ☐ Yes ☐ No

☐ Multi-factor authentication on financial accounts? ☐ Yes ☐ No ☐ Partial

☐ Multi-factor authentication on email? ☐ Yes ☐ No

☐ Wire transfer verification protocol established with advisors? ☐ Yes ☐ No

☐ Family members trained on phishing/scam recognition? ☐ Yes ☐ No

Notes: ____

Digital Footprint

☐ Searched yourself online in past year? ☐ Yes ☐ No

☐ Requested removal from data broker sites? ☐ Yes ☐ No

☐ Social media privacy settings reviewed? ☐ Yes ☐ No

☐ Location sharing disabled on social platforms? ☐ Yes ☐ No

Notes: ____

☐ Own property outside United States? ☐ Yes ☐ No

☐ If yes, local coverage in place for each property? ☐ Yes ☐ No ☐ Partial

☐ Travel internationally more than twice per year? ☐ Yes ☐ No

☐ Annual travel medical/evacuation policy in place? ☐ Yes ☐ No

☐ Umbrella policy provides worldwide coverage? ☐ Yes ☐ No ☐ Uncertain

☐ Travel to high-risk destinations? ☐ Yes ☐ No → Kidnap & Ransom coverage considered?

☐ Yes ☐ No

☐ Operate watercraft/aircraft internationally? ☐ Yes ☐ No → Coverage verified? ☐ Yes ☐ No

Notes: ____

☐ Primary insurance advisor: ______________________ Firm: __________________

☐ Advisor specializes in high-net-worth clients? ☐ Yes ☐ No ☐ Uncertain

☐ Access to private client carriers (Chubb, PURE, Cincinnati, Berkley One, Selective, Private Client Select)? ☐ Yes ☐ No ☐ Uncertain

☐ Last comprehensive review date: __________________

☐ Annual reviews conducted? ☐ Yes ☐ No

☐ Satisfied with responsiveness? ☐ Yes ☐ No

☐ Advisor proactively identifies gaps? ☐ Yes ☐ No

Notes: ____

Specialist Advisors (if applicable)

☐ Marine broker: ______________________

☐ Aviation broker: ______________________

☐ Fine art specialist: ______________________

☐ International specialist: ______________________

Notes: ____

Based on this audit, list the top issues requiring immediate attention:

1.
____

2.
____

3.
____

4.
____

5.
____

Next Steps:

☐ Schedule advisor meeting to review findings

☐ Request copies of all current policies for review

☐ Gather documentation for items needing to be scheduled

☐ Obtain updated appraisals where needed

From Fortified: The Affluent's Guide to Protecting Wealth, Lifestyle, and Legacy by Benjamin Walker
Additional resources at www.fortifiedbook.com

Annual Review
Preparation Checklist

This checklist helps prepare you for your annual insurance review. It covers what documents to gather, what changes to report since your last review, and what questions to bring. A productive review requires preparation from both sides — this ensures you hold up your end.

A fillable PDF version is available at www.fortifiedbook.com/resources.

ANNUAL REVIEW PREPARATION CHECKLIST

Making Your Insurance Review Count

A well-prepared client gets better protection than a passive one. Use this checklist to prepare for your annual insurance review. Complete it before your meeting so you arrive ready to have substantive conversations about your coverage.

Review Date: _______________________   Advisor: _________________________

PART 1: CHANGES SINCE LAST REVIEW

Property Changes

☐ Purchased or sold any real estate? If yes: ____

☐ Completed any renovations or improvements over $25,000? Details: ___________________

☐ Changed how any property is used? (Started renting, converted to home office, etc.)

☐ Added any structures (pool house, guest house, detached garage, etc.)?

☐ Any planned renovations in the next 12 months?

☐ Added or removed any safety or security features?

Vehicle Changes

☐ Purchased or sold any vehicles? Details: ____

☐ Added any recreational vehicles (boats, ATVs, motorcycles, etc.)?

☐ Any changes to who drives your vehicles (new teen driver, new employee)?

☐ Any changes to collector/classic vehicle values?

Valuables & Collections

☐ Acquired any significant jewelry, art, wine, or collectibles? Est. value: _______________

☐ Sold or gifted any previously scheduled items?

☐ Had any appraisals updated?

☐ Values of any collections changed significantly?

Household & Staff

☐ Hired or terminated any household employees?

☐ Changed employment arrangements (full-time to part-time, live-out to live-in)?

☐ Any changes to household composition (births, adult children moved out, etc.)?

Liability & Lifestyle

☐ Significant change in net worth? Approximate current net worth: ___________________

☐ Joined or left any boards (corporate, nonprofit, HOA)?

☐ Started any new business ventures or investments?

☐ Any increase in public profile (media coverage, speaking, awards)?

☐ Added any high-liability features (pool, trampoline, dog, horse)?

International

☐ Purchased property outside the US?

☐ Spending significantly more time internationally?

☐ Planning to travel to any high-risk destinations?

Annual Review Preparation Checklist

PART 2: QUESTIONS TO ASK YOUR ADVISOR

Coverage Adequacy

☐ Are my home reconstruction values current? When were they last updated?

☐ Does my umbrella limit still make sense given my current net worth?

☐ Are there any sub-limits I should be aware of that might be inadequate?

☐ Are all my valuables properly scheduled with current values?

Gaps & Exposures

☐ Are there any coverage gaps you've identified in my program?

☐ Given the changes I've described, are there new exposures I should address?

☐ Am I missing any coverage that families like mine typically have?

☐ Is my cyber coverage adequate? Do I even have cyber coverage?

Carriers & Markets

☐ Is my current carrier still the best fit, or should we look at alternatives?

☐ Have there been any changes in the market that affect my coverage options?

☐ Are there new products or coverage enhancements I should consider?

Premium & Value

☐ Are there any discounts or credits I'm not currently receiving?

☐ Would adjusting deductibles meaningfully change my premiums?

☐ Am I taking advantage of carrier risk management services?

Risk Reduction

☐ Are there risk reduction measures that would improve my coverage or lower premiums?

☐ Should I schedule a carrier risk assessment for any of my properties?

PART 3: DOCUMENTS TO BRING OR HAVE ACCESSIBLE

☐ Current policy declarations pages (if not already with advisor)

☐ Recent appraisals for jewelry, art, or other valuables

☐ Documentation for any new acquisitions

☐ Recent photos/video of properties (especially after renovations)

☐ List of household employees with hours and wages

☐ Information on any new vehicles or recreational equipment

☐ Recent financial statement or net worth summary

☐ List of current board positions

PART 4: MY SPECIFIC QUESTIONS & CONCERNS

List any specific questions or concerns you want to address:

1. ____

2. ____

3. ____

4. ____

5. ____

PART 5: POST-MEETING ACTION ITEMS

Record action items from your meeting:

☐ _______________________________________ Due: ____________

☐ _______________________________________ Due: ____________

☐ _______________________________________ Due: ____________

☐ _______________________________________ Due: ____________

☐ _______________________________________ Due: ____________

Next review scheduled for: _______________________________

Liability Adequacy Calculator

This worksheet helps you evaluate whether your umbrella liability limits match your actual exposure. It walks through the factors that should inform your coverage — net worth, property exposures, vehicles, household staff, public profile, and lifestyle risks — and provides a framework for the conversation with your advisor. There's no formula that produces a "correct" number, but most families carry far less than their risk profile warrants. This gives you a starting point. Coverage recommendations reflect your exposure profile, not carrier availability — actual limits offered will vary based on individual underwriting.

A fillable PDF version is available at www.fortifiedbook.com/resources.

LIABILITY ADEQUACY CALCULATOR

Evaluating Whether Your Umbrella Coverage Matches Your Exposure

This worksheet helps you think through the factors that should inform your umbrella liability limits. It's not a formula—there's no algorithm that produces a "correct" number. But it provides a framework for the conversation with your advisor.

STEP 1: BASELINE - NET WORTH

Your net worth is the starting point. In litigation, visible wealth makes you a target worth pursuing.

Approximate Net Worth (liquid + illiquid assets) $ ___________________

Current Umbrella Liability Limit $ ___________________

Baseline Umbrella Recommendation:

Net Worth $5M or Under	**Net Worth Over $5M**
$5M Umbrella Baseline	$10M Umbrella Baseline

My baseline umbrella recommendation: ☐ $5M ☐ $10M

Note: This baseline is your starting point. The exposure multipliers below may indicate you need coverage above this baseline.

STEP 2: EXPOSURE MULTIPLIERS

Certain factors increase your liability exposure beyond baseline. Check all that apply:

Property-Related Exposures

☐ Swimming pool (substantial drowning/injury risk)
☐ Multiple properties (each property = additional exposure)
☐ Rental properties (landlord liability)
☐ Waterfront property (drowning risk, attractive nuisance)
☐ Trampoline or play equipment
☐ Dogs (any breed, but especially breeds with bite history)
☐ Horses or other large animals
☐ Regular entertaining/events at home

Vehicle-Related Exposures

☐ Teen drivers in household (significantly elevated risk)
☐ Multiple vehicles
☐ High-performance vehicles
☐ Motorcycles
☐ Watercraft (boats, jet skis)
☐ Aircraft
☐ ATVs, snowmobiles, or other recreational vehicles
☐ Employees who drive your vehicles

Household & Employment Exposures

☐ Household employees (housekeeper, nanny, gardener, etc.)
☐ Live-in employees
☐ Estate manager or multiple staff

Professional & Public Profile

☐ Board service (corporate, nonprofit, HOA)
☐ Business ownership or significant investments
☐ Public profile (media coverage, speaking engagements)
☐ Active on social media with significant following

Liability Adequacy Calculator

☐ Profession with personal liability exposure

STEP 3: ASSESSMENT

Count your checked items:

0-3 items	4-8 items	9+ items
Standard exposure	Elevated exposure	High exposure
Baseline may be adequate	Consider 1.5x baseline	Consider 2x+ baseline

STEP 4: REALITY CHECK

Consider these questions:

- If a catastrophic accident occurred tomorrow, what's the worst-case judgment you could face?
- Are you comfortable with the gap between your current coverage and that scenario?
- How would an excess judgment affect your family's financial security?
- What's the marginal cost of additional coverage versus the peace of mind it provides?

STEP 5: DISCUSSION POINTS FOR YOUR ADVISOR

Based on this analysis, my liability profile is: ☐ Standard ☐ Elevated ☐ High

My baseline (from Step 1): ☐ $5M ☐ $10M

Suggested coverage based on profile: $ _______________________

Gap from current coverage: $ _____________________

Questions for advisor: ____

____

Important: This worksheet provides a thinking framework, not a recommendation. Your specific situation may warrant coverage different from these general guidelines. Discuss with a qualified advisor who understands your complete picture. Coverage calculations reflect your exposure profile, not carrier availability. Actual limits offered will vary based on individual underwriting criteria.

Acknowledgments

No book is written alone, even when it feels that way at 2 a.m., staring at a blinking cursor.

First, to my wife Amanda: you listened to me talk about this book far more than anyone should have to. You encouraged me when the words wouldn't come, celebrated with me when they did, and never once complained about the evenings and weekends I spent writing instead of being present. This book exists because you believed it should. I love you.

Furthermore, I couldn't have survived in this business without you. In our first year, every nickel went back into the business. If you hadn't been working your tail off, we would not have survived.

To my children — Adam, Sam, Tristan, Ashton, Quinn, and Oliver — you are the reason I care so deeply about protecting what families build. Watching you grow has taught me more about legacy than any textbook ever could.

To Pam, my co-founder and partner at Custom Insurance Solutions for nearly a decade: we built something together that I'm genuinely proud of. You tied your horse to mine, not knowing if we could make it work together, but trusting in me as I trusted in you. Your partnership, integrity, and friendship shaped everything that followed. Enjoy your well-earned retirement — you've earned every moment of it.

To my sister Kathi, who first told me about an open insurance agent position at AAA and unknowingly changed the trajectory of my life: thank you for that conversation. I owe my career to you. Without you, I may still be going home from work smelling of movie theater popcorn.

To the team at Custom Insurance Solutions: you guys are exceptional! Thank you for holding down the fort while I disappeared into chapters and revisions. Your dedication to our clients made it possible for me to step away and write, and I couldn't be prouder of you all!

To the colleagues and insurance industry professionals who inspire me. Bob Klee, Linda Fischer, Chris Paradiso, Daniel Seong, Bill Butler, David Carothers, Aron Robertson, Bradley Flowers, Scott Howell, Terren Moore, Rob Bowen, Erin Neill, Mike Stromsoe, Susan Shaw, Diane Delaney, Angela Lowrey, Rob Foshee, Maura Perkins, Glenn Berry, Jaren Harmon, Monica Jacob, Cindy Butler, Genevieve Hawkes, Matt Gordon, Micki Weber, and so many others who have shared their wisdom with me over the years, encouraged me, and continue to support me, your generosity improved these pages.

To the clients who have trusted me with their stories over the years: this book exists because of you. I've changed names and details throughout to protect your privacy, but the lessons are real. Thank you for letting me learn alongside you and for allowing your experiences to help others.

And finally, to everyone who picked up this book hoping to better protect what they've built: thank you for your trust. I hope these pages give you the clarity, confidence, and the strong risk management foundation you deserve. Now go have that conversation with your advisor — or find a better one.

Glossary

Key Terms for Understanding Risk Management and Insurance

Actual Cash Value (ACV) Replacement cost minus depreciation — what the item was worth at the time of loss, not what it costs to replace new.

Additional Insured A person or entity added to an insurance policy to receive coverage under it. Used when LLCs or trusts hold assets, or when requiring contractors to extend coverage to you.

Additional Living Expense (Loss of Use) Coverage for temporary housing and increased costs when your home is uninhabitable due to a covered loss. May be capped or unlimited (actual loss sustained).

Agreed Value A valuation method where you and the carrier agree on an item's value in advance. In a total loss, that amount is paid without negotiation or depreciation.

Attractive Nuisance A dangerous property feature (pool, trampoline, tree house) that may attract children too young to appreciate the risk. You may be liable for injuries even to trespassing children.

Blanket Coverage Insurance covering a category of items as a whole rather than individually. Used for large collections where scheduling every piece is impractical, typically with per-item caps within the overall limit.

Bodily Injury Physical harm to a person, including sickness, disease, or death. Distinguished from property damage (physical property) and personal injury (non-physical harm such as defamation).

Buy-Sell Agreement A binding agreement between business co-owners governing what happens to a partner's share upon death, disability, or departure. Often funded by life insurance.

Certificate of Insurance A document proving that coverage exists. Request these from contractors before work begins to verify they carry adequate liability and workers' compensation coverage.

COBRA Federal law allowing employees to continue health insurance after leaving employment. Household employers may have COBRA notification obligations when terminating employees.

Collections Policy A standalone policy designed to cover valuable collections such as fine art, jewelry, wine, or watches. Offers broader coverage, higher limits, and specialized claims handling compared with scheduling items on a homeowners policy.

Cyber Insurance (Personal) Coverage addressing digital risks, including financial fraud, identity theft restoration, cyber extortion (ransomware), privacy breach response, and related legal fees.

Deductible The amount you pay out of pocket before insurance kicks in. Higher deductibles, lower premiums — a form of intentional risk retention.

Depreciation The decrease in an item's value over time due to age, wear, and obsolescence. Subtracted from replacement cost under ACV coverage; eliminated under agreed value coverage.

Directors and Officers (D&O) Insurance Liability coverage for individuals serving on corporate or nonprofit boards. Typically has eroding limits, meaning defense costs reduce the coverage available for judgments.

Dwelling Coverage The portion of a homeowners policy covering the cost to repair or rebuild your home's physical structure. Should reflect actual reconstruction cost, not market value.

Employment Practices Liability (EPL) Insurance Coverage protecting employers against claims of wrongful termination, discrimination, harassment, retaliation, or other employment-related misconduct.

Endorsement A written amendment to an insurance policy that adds, removes, or modifies coverage.

Eroding Limits A policy feature where defense costs reduce total coverage available for judgments or settlements. If $500,000 is spent on defense, only the remaining limit is available for any judgment.

Excess Liability Coverage Additional liability coverage above primary policies. Similar to umbrella coverage but may have narrower terms. Used to build higher limits when a single carrier can't provide enough.

Exclusion A policy provision eliminating coverage for

specific risks or losses. Every exclusion represents a risk you're retaining, whether you realize it or not.

Extended Replacement Cost Coverage paying 25–50% above the stated dwelling limit if reconstruction costs exceed the policy amount. Better than basic limits but less protective than guaranteed replacement cost.

Fair Labor Standards Act (FLSA) Federal law governing minimum wage, overtime, and employment standards. Applies to household employees just as to business employees.

Floater (Personal Articles Floater) A policy or endorsement covering specific valuable items wherever they go — worldwide, not just at home.

Flood Insurance Separate coverage for flood damage, which is excluded from standard homeowners policies. Available through the NFIP or private insurers.

Form I-9 Federal form verifying employment eligibility. Required for every employee, including household employees, regardless of citizenship.

Guaranteed Replacement Cost The gold standard in property coverage. The carrier pays whatever it actually costs to rebuild, regardless of whether costs exceed the stated limit.

Hazard A condition that increases the likelihood or severity of a loss. Physical hazards include icy walkways or faulty wiring; moral hazards involve attitudes or behaviors that increase risk.

Homeowners Policy Coverage for owner-occupied residences, typically including dwelling, personal property, liability, and additional living expenses. Standard policies may be inadequate for high-value homes.

Hull Value In aviation and marine insurance, the agreed value of the aircraft or vessel itself. A primary factor in determining coverage and premiums.

Irrevocable Trust A trust that cannot be modified without the beneficiary's permission. Provides asset protection because the grantor has relinquished control.

Jones Act (Merchant Marine Act of 1920) Federal law protecting crew members injured on vessels. Creates liability for boat owners who employ crew, requiring specialized coverage.

Key Person Insurance Life or disability coverage taken out by a business on someone whose loss would significantly impact the company. Proceeds offset disruption and fund transitions.

Kidnap and Ransom (K&R) Insurance Coverage for kidnapping, extortion, and wrongful detention, including ransom payments and crisis response specialists.

Landlord Policy Insurance for properties rented to tenants. Replaces loss of use with loss of rental income and provides minimal personal property coverage.

Liability Limits The maximum an insurance policy will pay for liability claims, expressed as per-occurrence and aggregate limits. Essential because liability exposure is potentially unlimited.

Loss Damage, destruction, or disappearance of insured property, or a liability event triggering coverage. May be total or partial.

Loss of Rental Income Landlord policy coverage reimbursing lost rent when a rental property becomes uninhabitable due to a covered loss.

Loss of Use (Additional Living Expense) See Additional Living Expense.

Medical Evacuation Coverage Travel insurance for emergency medical transportation. Can cost $50,000–$250,000+ without insurance, making it essential for international travelers.

Medical Payments Coverage (Med Pay) Coverage paying medical expenses for people injured on your property or in your vehicle, regardless of fault. Typically $1,000–$10,000 in limits.

Misrepresentation A false statement in an insurance application or claim. Material misrepresentation can void a policy entirely.

Multi-Factor Authentication (MFA) A security practice requiring two or more verification methods to access an account — typically a password plus a phone or security key.

Mysterious Disappearance Coverage for items that vanish without explanation — no evidence of theft, no witnesses. Important because professional thieves often leave no evidence.

Nanny Tax Employment taxes (Social Security and Medicare) that household employers must withhold and pay for domestic employees earning above the IRS threshold.

Navigational Limits Geographic boundaries within which marine insurance applies. Operating beyond them without carrier approval can void coverage entirely.

Negligence Failure to exercise reasonable care, resulting in harm to another. The basis for most liability claims.

Negligent Entrustment Legal doctrine holding you liable

for lending a dangerous item (such as a vehicle) to someone you knew or should have known was likely to use it unsafely.

Nuclear Verdict Industry term for jury verdicts exceeding $10 million. Increasingly common, particularly against defendants with visible wealth.

Other Structures Coverage Homeowners policy coverage for structures separate from the main dwelling — garages, pool houses, guest houses, fences. Should reflect actual reconstruction costs.

Peril A specific cause of loss (fire, theft, windstorm, water damage). Policies cover either named perils (only those listed) or open perils (all causes except those excluded).

Personal Property Coverage Homeowners policy coverage for belongings — furniture, clothing, electronics. Subject to sub-limits for categories like jewelry, art, and wine.

Phishing Fraudulent emails, texts, or calls impersonating legitimate senders to steal credentials or prompt unauthorized actions. The most common entry point for cyber attacks.

Premium The amount paid for insurance coverage. Reflects the carrier's assessment of risk.

Private Client Carriers Insurers specializing in high-networth coverage, offering broader forms, higher limits, specialized claims handling, and risk management services unavailable from standard carriers.

Punitive Damages Damages intended to punish egregious conduct, beyond compensating the plaintiff. Many umbrella policies exclude these, meaning you pay out of pocket.

Reconstruction Cost What it would actually cost to rebuild a property using similar materials and craftsmanship. Often differs from market value. Should be professionally appraised.

Rental Reimbursement Coverage Auto coverage for rental vehicles while yours is being repaired. Standard policies often cap at $30–50/day for 30 days — potentially inadequate for specialty vehicles.

Revocable Trust A trust modifiable by the grantor during their lifetime. Useful for estate planning but provides little asset protection. See also Irrevocable Trust.

Risk Advisor An insurance professional who analyzes overall exposure and designs comprehensive protection, rather than simply selling policies.

Risk Avoidance One of the Four Pillars. Declining to take on certain risks — choosing not to add a diving board, lend your car, or rent your vacation home.

Risk Reduction One of the Four Pillars. Actions decreasing the likelihood or severity of losses — maintenance, protective systems, training, documentation.

Risk Retention One of the Four Pillars. Consciously accepting responsibility for certain risks — deductibles, self-insuring smaller exposures, and understanding that some risks can't be fully transferred.

Risk Transfer One of the Four Pillars. Shifting financial responsibility to another party through insurance, contracts, or legal structures.

Schedule H The IRS form household employers file to report employment taxes for domestic employees.

SIM Swapping Fraud where criminals convince your carrier to transfer your phone number to their device, intercepting calls, texts, and authentication codes.

Social Engineering Manipulation techniques deceiving people into revealing information or taking actions that compromise security. Most cyber attacks succeed this way rather than through technical hacking.

Spoilage Coverage Coverage for perishable items damaged by temperature or humidity failures. Critical for wine collections. Not always included automatically.

Sub-Limit A cap on coverage for specific property categories within a broader limit. Your policy might have $2 million in personal property coverage but only a $10,000 sub-limit for jewelry.

Total Loss Complete destruction of insured property, or damage where repair costs exceed value. The insurer pays the policy limit or agreed value.

Umbrella Policy Liability coverage above the limits of underlying policies (auto, homeowners, watercraft). Often includes broader protection for situations underlying policies exclude.

Underlying Policy The primary policies (auto, homeowners, watercraft) beneath umbrella coverage. The umbrella requires these to maintain minimum limits and pays only after they're exhausted.

Underwriting The process insurers use to evaluate risk and determine coverage terms. Factors include property characteristics, claims history, and personal profile.

Uninsured/Underinsured Motorist Coverage (UM/UIM) Protection when you're injured by a driver who lacks insurance or has insufficient coverage. Should match your liability limits.

W-2 Tax form showing wages paid and taxes withheld. Household employers must issue W-2s to domestic employees by January 31 each year.

Wire Fraud Schemes redirecting legitimate wire transfers to criminal accounts through compromised email or impersonation. Among the most financially devastating cyber threats.

Workers' Compensation Insurance Coverage for employees injured on the job — medical expenses, rehabilitation, and wage replacement. In exchange, employees generally give up the right to sue. Required for household employees in many states.

About the Author

Ben Walker, CPRM, CPRIA, is the founder of Custom Insurance Solutions, an insurance agency dedicated to helping affluent clients build comprehensive risk management portfolios across all 50 states and the District of Columbia. Ben and his team of licensed professionals provide comprehensive risk assessments, ongoing stewardship, and advocacy for their clients. Since founding the agency in 2011, Ben has built his practice on a highly consultative and collaborative approach — getting to know his clients, understanding their unique exposures, and serving as their advocate when it matters most. Ben and his team work closely with wealth managers, family offices, and estate attorneys to ensure their clients are properly protected.

Ben lives in Highland, Utah with his wife, Amanda, and their children. He enjoys golf and welcomes any excuse to get out on the course. When he's not advising clients or avoiding three-putts, Ben can be found enjoying movies and live theater, woodworking and welding, or traveling with his family.

About CIS Private Client

CIS Private Client is the private client division of Custom Insurance Solutions, specializing in risk management for high-net-worth and ultra-high-net-worth individuals and families. Our services include comprehensive risk assessments, ongoing stewardship of your insurance portfolio, access to private client carriers, and coordination with your other trusted advisors. We know this niche inside and out, and we bring that expertise to every client relationship.

Certified Personal Risk Manager (CPRM)

The CPRM designation is awarded by the National Alliance for Insurance Education & Research to professionals who demonstrate advanced expertise in identifying, analyzing, and managing the personal risks faced by high-net-worth individuals and families. The program covers property, liability, life, and health exposures unique to affluent clients.

Certified Personal Risk and Insurance Advisor (CPRIA)

The CPRIA designation is conferred by the Private Risk Management Association (PRMA) and recognizes professionals who have demonstrated specialized expertise in serving the insurance and risk management needs of affluent clients, including coverage analysis, carrier selection, and client advocacy.

Get in Touch

To learn more or to schedule a consultation:

Phone: 801-701-7007

Email: Ben@MyCustomInsurance.com

Website: www.MyCustomInsurance.com

9 798994 054307